**Sexual Assault
among
Adolescents**

Sexual Assault among Adolescents

Suzanne S. Ageton
Behavioral Research
Institute

Lexington Books
D.C. Heath and Company
Lexington, Massachusetts
Toronto

Library of Congress Cataloging in Publication Data

Ageton, Suzanne S.
  Sexual assault among adolescents.

  Bibliography: p.
  Includes index.
  1. Rape victims—United States—Longitudinal studies. 2. Rapists—United States—Longitudinal studies. 3. Youth—Sexual behavior—Longitudinal studies. 4. Sex crimes—United States—Longitudinal studies. I. Title.
HV6561.A4   1983   364.1′532   82-48573
ISBN 0-669-06322-3

Copyright © 1983 by D.C. Heath and Company

All rights reserved. No part of this publication may be reproduced or transmitted in any form or by any means, electronic or mechanical, including photocopy, recording, or any information storage or retrieval system, without permission in writing from the publisher.

Published simultaneously in Canada

Printed in the United States of America

International Standard Book Number: 0-669-06322-3

Library of Congress Catalog Card Number: 82-48573

Contents

	Tables	ix
	Acknowledgments	xi
Part I	*Background and Methodology*	1
Chapter 1	**Introduction**	3
Chapter 2	**Research Methods and Procedures**	7
	Research Design	7
	The Sample	7
	Validity of the Data	12
	Description of the Data Base	18
	General Analytical Approach	20
Part II	*The Adolescent Victim*	23
Chapter 3	**The Nature and Extent of Sexual Assault among Adolescent Females, 1978–1980**	25
	Prevalence and Incidence Estimates	25
	Comparisons with Uniform Crime Reports and the National Crime Survey	29
	Comparison of Victim Profiles	33
	Probability of Being Sexually Assaulted	35
Chapter 4	**The Sexual-Assault Experience from the Victim's Perspective**	39
	Circumstances of a Sexual Assault	39
	Offender Characteristics	40
	Force and Pressure Experienced	41
	Victim Resistance and Outcome	43
	Summary	44
Chapter 5	**The Aftermath of Sexual Assault**	47
	Reports to the Police	47
	Effects on Personal Relationships	48
	Effects on Personal Behavior	51
	Initial Reactions	52

v

	First Follow-up	54
	Differential Response to a Sexual Assault	55
	Long-Term Reactions to a Sexual Assault	59
Chapter 6	**Vulnerability to Sexual Assault**	65
	Conceptualization of Vulnerability	67
	Analysis Procedures	69
	Victim and Control-Group Comparisons, 1978–1980	70
	Previctimization Comparisons	77
	Are Sexual-Assault Victims Unique among Assault Victims?	80
Part III	*The Adolescent Offender*	83
Chapter 7	**The Nature and Extent of Sexual Assault Committed by Adolescent Males, 1978–1980**	85
	Prevalence and Incidence Estimates	85
	Comparisons with Uniform Crime Reports and the National Crime Survey	89
	Comparison of Offender Profiles	91
Chapter 8	**The Sexual-Assault Experience from the Offender's Perspective**	95
	Circumstances of a Sexual Assault	95
	Victim Characteristics	98
	Reactions to a Sexual Assault	99
	Summary	99
Chapter 9	**Prediction of Adolescent Sexual-Assault Offenders**	101
	Sexual-Assault Model	101
	Analysis Procedures	105
	Offender and Control-Group Comparisons, 1978–1980	106
	Pre-Sexual-Assault Comparisons	112
	Multivariate Assessment of the Integrated Delinquency Model	115
	Test of the Sexual-Assault Model	116
	Conclusions	120

Contents

Part IV		An Overview of Adolescent Sexual Assault	125
Chapter 10		**Summary of Major Findings**	127
		Prevalence and Incidence Estimates for Victims	127
		Comparisons of the Sexual Assault Project, National Crime Survey, and Uniform Crime Reports	128
		The Sexual-Assault Experience from the Victim's View	129
		The Aftermath of Sexual Assault	130
		Differential Response to a Sexual Assault	131
		Long-Term Reactions to a Sexual Assault	131
		Vulnerability to Sexual Assault	132
		Prevalence and Incidence Estimates for Offenders	133
		Profiles of Adolescent Offenders	134
		The Sexual-Assault Experience from the Offender's View	135
		Prediction of Adolescent Sexual-Assault Offenders	136
Chapter 11		**Issues and Directions for Sexual-Assault Research**	139
		Appendix A: Description of Attitudinal and Behavioral Scales	143
		Appendix B: Scale Reliabilities	149
		Appendix C: Sexual-Assault Questions	153
		Bibliography	171
		Glossary	179
		Index of Names	183
		About the Author	185

Tables

2–1	Sample Sizes for Female Victims and Male Offenders	11
3–1	Proportion of Female Youth Reporting One or More Sexual Assaults by Age, Social Class, Race, and Place of Residence, 1978–1980	26
3–2	Average Number of Sexual Assaults per Female by Age, Social Class, Race, and Place of Residence, 1978–1980	28
3–3	Rape and Sexual-Assault Rates for Females, per 1,000 Population	31
4–1	Proportion of Victims Reporting Each Type of Force, 1978–1980	41
4–2	Proportion of Victims Who Reported Each Type of Force as the Most Serious They Experienced, 1978–1980	42
5–1	Proportion of Victims Who Reported Each Reaction within a Week of a Sexual Assault, 1978–1980	53
5–2	Proportion of Victims Reporting Each Reaction from One to Twelve Months after a Sexual Assault, 1978–1980	55
5–3	Proportion of 1978 Victims Reporting Each Reaction at Four Time Periods after a Sexual Assault	59
6–1	Significant Mean ($\bar{X}$) Differences between Victims and Controls on Self-Report Delinquency and Victimization Scales, 1978	71
6–2	Significant Mean ($\bar{X}$) Differences between Victims and Controls on Attitudinal and Behavioral Scales, 1979	72
6–3	Significant Mean ($\bar{X}$) Differences between Victims and Controls on Attitudinal and Behavioral Scales, 1980	74
6–4	Mean Differences between Future Sexual-Assault Victims (V) and Controls (C) on Selected Attitudinal Scales	78

7–1	Proportion of Male Youth Who Report Committing One or More Sexual Assaults by Age, Social Class, Race, and Place of Residence, 1978–1980	86
7–2	Average Number of Sexual Assaults Committed per Male by Age, Social Class, Race, and Place of Residence, 1978–1980	87
8–1	Proportion of Offenders Reporting Use of Each Type of Force, 1978–1980	96
8–2	Proportion of Offenders Who Reported Each Type of Force as the Most Serious They Used, 1978–1980	97
9–1	Significant Mean ($\bar{X}$) Differences between Offenders and Nonoffenders on Peer Variables, 1978	107
9–2	Significant Mean ($\bar{X}$) Differences between Offenders and Nonoffenders on Attitudinal and Behavioral Scales, 1979	109
9–3	Significant Mean ($\bar{X}$) Differences between Offenders and Nonoffenders on Attitudinal and Behavioral Scales, 1980	111
9–4	Mean Differences between Future Sexual-Assault Offenders (O) and Controls (C) on Selected Attitudinal Scales	114
B–1	Scale Reliabilities and Homogeneity Ratios	149
B–2	Reliability Indexes for Various Self-Report Delinquency Scales	151

Acknowledgments

This work was supported by two grants from the Center for the Prevention and Control of Rape, National Institute of Mental Health (NIMH) (MH 31751), for the period July 1978 through January 1983. The National Youth Survey was supported by a series of grants from the Center for Studies of Crime and Delinquency, NIHM (MH 27552), for the period June 1975 through May 1983. The points of view or opinions expressed in this book are, of course, mine.

To those young sexual-assault victims and offenders who shared their experiences with us, I extend my special thanks. Their willingness to describe a personal and possibly stressful event in their lives provides valuable information on adolescent sexual assault.

The success of any research effort in large measure is dependent on the quality of the staff. I was fortunate in the skill, commitment, and energy that members of my staff brought to their jobs. I would like to recognize the multiple contributions of my research associate, Rachelle Canter; my research analysts, Linda Hill and Ann Riley; and my research assistant, Nancy Andes. Able and efficient clerical support was provided throughout the research by Pam McElroy, Charlotte Nelson, Joannie Cradick, and Phyllis O'Meara.

I owe a debt of special gratitude to David Huizinga for his continual and invaluable advice on methodological issues. The counsel and suggestions of Delbert Elliott on various drafts are also greatly appreciated. Finally, my particular thanks go to Rex, Christine, and Brett, three special people in my life whose support and love kept me going.

Part I
Background and Methodology

1 Introduction

Over the past decade, criminal-justice and social-science research has indicated that adolescents are the victims and perpetrators of a fair amount of sexual violence. A national survey of junior- and senior-high-school students reported a 40 percent increase in rapes committed in school from 1970 to 1973 (U.S. Congress 1977). Consistently throughout the 1970s, National Crime Survey data showed that youth aged sixteen through nineteen had the highest or next-to-highest rate of rape of the seven age classifications surveyed (U.S. Department of Justice 1980). A large study of reported rape victims in Philadelphia (McCahill, Meyer, and Fischman 1979) confirmed the predominance of teenagers among rape victims. In addition, Katz and Mazur (1979) in their extensive review of rape research noted that adolescents constituted the largest group of sexual-assault victims reported to the police.

Adolescents also feature prominently in statistics on sexual-assault offenders. The findings of a report on major violent crimes in several American cities (Curtis 1974) show that in over 50 percent of the reported rapes, the victim, the offender, or both were adolescents. Throughout the late 1970s, Uniform Crime Reports consistently showed that adolescents constituted a high proportion, often 30 percent or more, of those arrested for rape (U.S. Department of Justice 1977–1980). Innumerable smaller studies also support the conclusion that adolescents are disproportionately involved in sexual assault, as both victims and offenders (McCombie 1976; Peters, Meyers, and Carroll 1976; MacDonald 1971; Amir 1971; Hursch and Selkin 1974).

Despite what appear to be fairly extensive data on adolescent involvement in sexual assault, our knowledge of the magnitude and distribution of this behavior is limited in several ways. Most important, much of our information is based on samples of reported victims or known offenders, neither of which is a representative sample of all youth involved in sexual assault. Rape or sexual-assault cases reported to the police represent only a small portion of all such cases (Feldman-Summers 1975; Flanagan, van Alstyne, and Gottfredson 1982). Recent research has suggested that victims who report crimes are distinguishable from victims who do not on such variables as race and age (Greenberg and Wilson 1977). Furthermore the available data suggest that rapes involving known assailants may be substantially underrepresented in official statistics (Turner 1972; Catlin and Murray 1979). Dependence on only those rape and sexual-assault cases that come to the attention of the authorities is likely to bias the conclusions drawn. To describe accurately the involvement of youth in sexual assault requires data drawn from a representative sample of adolescents.

A second limitation to the existing research is the paucity of studies with longitudinal panel data, data from the same subjects for more than one time period. The general absence of these kinds of data means that information on the reoccurrence of sexual assault, the long-range consequences of sexual assault, or the behavioral and attitudinal patterns associated with becoming a sexual-assault victim or offender is very limited. Developmental data are critical to understanding both the occurrence of rape and its aftermath. Successful prevention strategies as well as those for treating victims and offenders are dependent on such information.

Although evidence has been available for some time that a high proportion of youth are sexually assaulted by friends or dates (Evrard and Gold 1979; Hayman et al. 1968; Schultz and DeSavage 1975; Kanin and Parcell 1977), these findings are tied to purposive samples, often composed of only college-age students. Data on the occurrence of nonstranger rape and sexual assault among teenagers are limited. Moreover, recent evidence suggests that basic survey questions on rape and sexual assault may not be capturing information on this kind of behavior. In a study of adolescent sexuality, it was discovered that many youth were reluctant to label as rape certain types of forced sex that occurred in the context of a date (Zellman et al., 1981). This reluctance held even if physical force was used. If this finding applies to most youth, standard queries about being raped or sexually assaulted will not elicit responses about what may be the most-common forced sexual behavior that adolescents encounter. Thus data gathered by the National Crime Surveys and those generated from most studies of forcible rape are not likely to reflect the occurrence of date rape among adolescents.

A final concern about the existing work on adolescent sexual assault applies to all rape and sexual-assault research. With few exceptions (for example, Sanday 1981; Williams and Holmes 1981), the study of rape and sexual assault has not been guided by theory. Most work in this field has been descriptive and atheoretical. Although a variety of sociological theories have been offered as relevant to the study of rape including conflict theory, attribution theory, and subcultural theory, too few researchers have moved beyond the conceptualization stage to test their ideas empirically.[1] Thus, there has been little theoretical development and advancement regarding the causes and consequences of rape and sexual assault.

Introduction

The Sexual Assault Project (SAP) described in this book was designed to address several of these concerns. First, a national probability sample of adolescents aged eleven through seventeen in 1976 was employed so that findings could be generalized to all youth in the same age range. National estimates of the annual incidence (frequency of occurrence) and prevalence (proportion of youth involved at least once) of sexual assault for both teenage victims and offenders may be generated from this sample. Furthermore, specific information was collected on the occurrence of sexually assaultive behavior within the context of a date. Overall data from this sample provide a more-representative picture of the magnitude and distribution of adolescent sexual assault than data from purposive samples.

Second, the design of the research involved interviewing the same group or panel of youth once a year for five consecutive years. Use of this longitudinal panel design rather than the traditional cross-sectional one allows extensive follow-up on adolescent victims. Questions about the persistence of reactions to an assault and long-term consequences for behavior and attitudes cannot be addressed without this type of design. In addition, five years of continuous data on the same subjects permits an examination of the process of becoming a sexual-assault victim or offender. The dynamics of these processes can be understood only with developmental data.

From a theoretical perspective, the research introduces a predictive model of adolescent sexual assault derived from delinquency theory. The relevance of a set of defined variables to the commission of sexual assault is evaluated both statically and dynamically. Furthermore, vulnerability to sexual assault is explored by systematically analyzing the circumstances and characteristics associated with becoming a sexual-assault victim. Although no precise theoretical model is proposed to predict vulnerability to sexual assault, the data are used to explore several general ideas about being sexually victimized, such as the postulated relationship between a deviant life-style and vulnerability to sexual assault.

Overall the intent of the SAP is to meet four specific objectives, two descriptive and two explanatory. The first descriptive goal is to provide nationally representative data on the incidence, prevalence, and distribution of sexual assault for adolescent victims and offenders. The second is to describe and assess victim reactions to sexual assault, both initially and over a period of one to three years after the assault. A descriptive profile of adolescent victims and offenders is also projected, along with a comprehensive depiction of the sexual-assault experience.

The primary explanatory objectives of the study are to develop and test a theoretical model of adolescent sexual assault and to explore the question of adolescent vulnerability to sexual assault. Both of these goals involve attempting to fit existing knowledge and beliefs about the causes and risks of sexual assault into conceptual frameworks and then empirically testing these frameworks with the SAP data.

This book has four major parts. Part I introduces the topic and provides detailed information on the research design, sample and methodology. Part II contains four chapters, each dealing with a separate aspect of the sexual-assault experience for the adolescent female victim. Chapter 3 documents the annual incidence, prevalence, and social correlates of sexual assault for the years 1978 through 1980. Chapters 4 and 5 describe the assault experience and the behavioral and attitudinal consequences of being sexually assaulted. Chapter 6 presents a conceptualization of vulnerability to sexual assault and tests this set of ideas with victim and control data.

Part III contains the adolescent offender data, with chapter 7 documenting the annual incidence, prevalence, and social correlates of sexual assault committed by teenage males for the years 1978 through 1980. Chapter 8 details the assault from the offender's perspective, as well as providing data on the offender's reactions to this incident. The prediction of adolescent sexual-assault offenders is dealt with in chapter 9 which also introduces an integrated theoretical model derived from delinquency theory. The relevance of this model to sexual-assault offenders is discussed and some modifications offered. The power of this model to discriminate sexual-assault offenders from nonoffenders is tested and assessed.

Part IV contains a general summary of findings and a broad discussion of some major issues facing sexual-assault research.

Note

1. For a review of sociological theories regarding rape and methodological concerns with existing research, refer to Deming and Eppy (1981).

2 Research Methods and Procedures

Research Design

The SAP grew out of a larger study on delinquent behavior, the National Youth Survey (NYS). The NYS uses a longitudinal, sequential design with multiple birth cohorts. The sample, selected in 1976, was a national-probability sample of youth aged eleven through seventeen and included seven birth cohorts (1959–1965). The total youth sample was interviewed initially between January and March 1977 concerning their victimization and involvement in delinquent behavior during the calendar year 1976. The second, third, fourth, and fifth surveys were conducted during these same months in successive years. By the fifth survey (1981), the panel was fifteen through twenty-one years of age. The cumulated data across the five years of the study cover the entire adolescent period.[1]

Because the original NYS interview contained self-reports of sexual assaults from both victims and offenders, the basic data were available from which to develop a more-comprehensive study of sexual assault among adolescents. Funding for the SAP began in 1978, and for the last three years of the NYS (1978 through 1980), specific information about any reported sexual assaults was obtained from all of the self-identified victims and offenders. These data plus the general attitudinal and behavioral data gathered in the NYS provided the basis for the nationally representative study of adolescent sexual assault presented in this book.

The Sample

The NYS Sample

The NYS employed a probability sample of households in the continental United States in 1976 based on a multistage, cluster-sampling design. At each stage, the probabilities of selection were established to provide a self-weighting sample. Seventy-six sampling units were selected, with probability of selection being proportional to size. Approximately 8,000 households were selected for inclusion in the sample, and all youth living in these households who were eleven through seventeen years of age on December 31, 1976, and were physically and mentally capable of being interviewed were eligible respondents for the study. Out of an estimated total of 2,360 eligible youth, 635 (27 percent) did not participate in the study due to parental refusal, youth refusal, or inability to establish contact with the respondent. The remaining 1,725 agreed to participate in the study, signed informed consents, and completed interviews in the initial survey (1977).

An age, sex, and race comparison of nonparticipating eligible youth and participating youth indicates that the initial loss rate from any particular age, sex, or racial group appears to be proportional to that group's representation in the population. Further, with respect to these characteristics, participating youth appear to be representative of the total eleven- through seventeen-year-old youth population in the United States as established by the U.S. Census Bureau.

Across the five years of the study, the total sample loss was 231 youth, or 13.4 percent of the original year 1 participants. Tests for selective loss on basic demographic characteristics suggest that although there was some selective loss over time with respect to race, class, and place of residence, the cumulative loss rates were very small. Overall there is no evidence that the participating samples for waves 2 through 5 lost their representativeness by sex, age, race, social class, or place of residence.

The Sexual-Assault Sample

For purposes of this research, sexual assault was defined to include all forced sexual behavior involving contact with the sexual parts of the body. Thus the definition could encompass forcible rape, incest, sodomy, and fondling but not exhibitionism or other sexual acts where no contact was established. Attempted sexual assaults were counted. In addition, we allowed the force component to be as mild as verbal pressure or as severe as a physical beating or injury from a weapon.

This relatively broad definition was chosen because of our interest in the range of forced sexual experiences among adolescents, specifically the so-called date rape.[2] We suspect that many adolescents experience forced contact with the sexual parts of their bodies that does not conclude with forceful sexual intercourse. Nonetheless many of these acts qualify as sexual assaults and may have significant implications for adolescents whose sexuality is just emerging. Limiting queries to forcible rapes would have excluded a priori all forced sexual acts that fell short of rape. Although this definition may bring in behaviors that are not sexual assaults, we believed a broad definition was necessary to capture the range of sexual assaults that adolescents experience.

Research Methods and Procedures

Out of the NYS sample, those respondents who self-identified as sexual-assault victims or offenders became the sexual-assault sample. This self-identification process had two stages. Initially each respondent was asked several questions to determine whether he or she had committed and/or experienced a possible sexual assault. These questions were embedded in a larger set of delinquency and victimization items. They were designed to cover the continuum of sexual-assault behavior from the stereotypic violent stranger assault to the date-rape situation. A response of one or more to any of the following questions tentatively placed the respondent in the sexual-assault sample. The first three questions were used to identify possible offenders and the remainder to identify victims.

How many times in the last year have you:
1. Had or tried to have sexual relations with someone against their will?
2. Pressured or pushed someone such as a date or friend to do more sexually than they wanted to do?
3. Physically hurt or threatened to hurt someone to get them to have sex with you?
4. Been sexually attacked or raped or an attempt made to do so?
5. Been pressured or pushed by someone such as a date or friend to do more sexually than you wanted to do?

In addition to the specific sexual-assault questions, reports of physical assaults were followed up to ascertain whether a sexual assault had occurred as well. If it had, these cases were added to the pool of potential victims.

This set of items represents a major expansion from the two items (one for victims and one for offenders) that were part of the original NYS survey (these are numbers 1 and 4 of the preceding list). The additional questions were asked in an attempt to broaden and specify the types of forced sexual behavior we wanted to include. Specifically we wanted to capture those forced sexual behaviors that occur in the context of a date but may not be defined as rape or even as sexual assault.

One drawback to this expansion was that we created overlap in the items and the possibility of multiple reports of the same incident. Therefore respondents were asked to tell us the total number of sexual assaults that had occurred during the year whenever more than one of the sexual-assault questions was answered. This procedure was able to provide a nonredundant count despite the overlapping questions.

The second stage in the self-identification process involved reading to all potential victims and offenders a general description of the sexual situations we were defining as sexual assaults. This second-level filter of potential sexual-assault cases was deemed necessary for two reasons. First, since the

SAP was essentially a secondary research effort tied to an ongoing study of delinquent behavior, the goals of the primary study had to be given priority. This meant that a detailed description of sexual assault and the gathering of precise information on what sexual behavior occurred during the assault were precluded for fear of jeopardizing respondent participation in the larger study. Consequently the presentation of a general description of sexual assault to all potential cases was judged critical to ensure that only legitimate cases were pursued. In addition, it was felt that the age of the sample might work against a clear understanding of the initial questions and that it would be wise to give all potential victims and offenders a consistent description of the behavior of interest. The reading of a general description would also permit respondents to deselect themselves before the questioning began if the behavior they had reported did not fit the description read to them.

The broad description of sexual assault, part of the general introduction to the specific sexual-assault questions, was read to all potential victims and offenders, and the wording for the victims is presented here. Obviously the wording is slightly different for potential offenders although the content is roughly the same.

> The following set of questions is related to the event you reported earlier in the interview of having been pressured by someone to do more sexually than you wanted to do. For purposes of this interview, we are interested in the sexual situation in which someone pressured you into contact with the private parts of your body or theirs. Please remember that all your answers are confidential and that your name will not appear anywhere on the interview.

Respondents who passed through both of these stages of the self-identification process were considered legitimate victims and/or offenders and were asked the special sexual-assault questions at the end of the regular interview. This process was followed for each of the three years described in this book.

Table 2-1 displays the number of female-victim and male-offender cases generated in 1978, 1979, and 1980. Although a few female offenders and male victims did appear in the sample, they are not included in the analyses presented because these cases are different from the majority sex cases in each group. To include them could result in misleading conclusions regarding the majority of adolescent sexual-assault victims and offenders. Homosexual assaults also were excluded because they do not conform to the typical case involving a female victim and a male offender.

The female-victim data in table 2-1 show that from 1978 through 1980, 172 completed interviews were obtained from female victims.[3] Approxi-

Table 2-1
Sample Sizes for Female Victims and Male Offenders

	1978	1979	1980
Female victims	66	72	52
Refusals[a]			1
Deselects[b]	2	9	4
Errors[c]	2		
Complete interviews	62	63	47
Male offenders	33	24	25
Refusals[a]	2		
Deselects[b]		1	8
Errors[c]	3		
Complete interviews	28	23	17

Notes: The 172 complete interviews from female victims 1978 through 1980 represent 135 individuals because a number of female victims reported in more than one of the three years. The 68 complete interviews from male offenders during the same years represent 51 individuals because a number of male offenders reported in more than one of the three years.
[a]Respondents who refused to answer the specific sexual-assault questions after self-identifying as a sexual-assault victim or offender.
[b]Respondents who indicated that the sexual assault reported when they self-identified did not qualify under the definition read to them prior to receiving the special sexual-assault questions.
[c]Respondents who self-identified as sexual-assault offenders or victims but were not asked the special questions due to interviewer error.

mately 20 cases were lost due to refusal, deselection, or interviewer error, with the majority lost by deselection. Most of these cases had responded to the date-rape item (they had been pressured or pushed by someone such as a date or friend to do more sexually than they had wanted to do). The respondents' comments regarding the general description of sexual assault read to them suggest that they interpreted the date-rape item more loosely than was intended. In almost all instances, these deselections seemed appropriate because the incident reported contained pressure for kissing and/or petting but no forced contact with the sexual parts of the body. Of course, it is not possible to know whether some of these deselections reflect lying to avoid questions about a legitimate sexual assault. Nonetheless respondent comments and interviewer observations suggest that the preponderance of the deselections were legitimate.

With regard to male offenders, the data in table 2-1 indicate that 68 completed interviews were obtained from 1978 through 1980.[4] Fourteen cases were lost due to refusal, interviewer error, or deselection, with deselection again accounting for the majority of the losses. The substantially smaller sample size for the offenders is not surprising inasmuch as it is based on self-reports of illegal and socially unacceptable behavior.

Validity of the Data

Whether the sexual-assault data accurately reflect the volume and distribution of this behavior among adolescents in the United States is a critical question. The credibility of the findings and general acceptance of the research depend on a comprehensive assessment of this issue. With regard to the victim data, two central concerns regarding the reporting of sexual assault will be discussed: nonresponse or nonreporting and inaccurate or incomplete recall. We review the relevant literature on these issues and discuss the implications of the findings for the sexual-assault victim data. For the offender data, we present some validation work conducted on all of the self-report delinquency scales form the NYS. A discussion of the validity and reliability of the self-report technique in general concludes this section.

Victim Reports

Concern with nonresponse has two separate issues: failure to remember and purposeful concealment of an incident. With regard to forgetting, it is generally accepted that victims forget crime incidents with the passage of time. This was noted in several pretests conducted by the U.S. Census Bureau as part of the development work preceding the National Crime Survey (Yost and Dodge 1970; Dodge 1970; Turner 1972). In these pretests, record checks were made in which samples of incidents were drawn from police files, and the victims subsequently were interviewed to discover whether they could recall and accurately remember the month of the incident. Declining rates of recall with the passage of time were observed in all these studies. For the San Jose study (Turner 1972), the rate of recall dropped more than 50 percent as the period between the incident and the interview increased from one to three months to ten to twelve months. On the other hand, a study in England (Sparks, Glenn, and Dodd 1977) noted high rates of recall and only a slight decline over a ten-month period. This study also was able to improve accuracy of recall by focusing the respondents on salient events in their lives and then locating victimizations within the context of these events.

Data on the correlates of forgetting, other than the passage of time, are limited and conflicting; however, findings from the record-check study in San Jose indicate that the nature of the victim-offender relationship influences the reporting of personal victimizations. While 76 percent of the incidents involving strangers were recalled, only 57 percent of those involving a known offender were. This percentage dropped to 22 percent when the offender was related to the victim. Comparable results were obtained in a record-check study of assaults conducted in Canada (Catlin and Murray

1979). While 71 percent of stranger assaults were recalled in this study, only 56 percent of those involving known assailants were and even fewer of those involving relatives (29 percent).

Of special significance in the San Jose study was the finding that eleven of the fifteen rapes that were not recalled involved nonstrangers. The overall rate of recall for rape incidents was 67 percent, but it was substantially higher for rapes involving strangers (84 percent). Whether these findings reflect memory decay, lying, or suppression of an incident the victim may feel guilty about is impossible to determine. Nonetheless they do suggest that rapes involving known assailants may be substantially underreported.

The effect of lying or purposeful nonreporting on victim reports is exceedingly hard to evaluate. As Skogan points out (1981:16), "The evidence that respondents may be lying, or deliberately suppressing reports of events of which they have full knowledge, is quite inferential." While the low recall of victimizations involving nonstrangers may be attributed to lying, competing explanations could be offered. Suppression of a painful experience, redefinition of an incident with the passage of time, or feelings of culpability may all inhibit reporting. Hard evidence of the magnitude of purposive concealment in victimization surveys is not available.

The second major concern regarding the validity of sexual-assault data is inaccurate or incomplete recall. This problem involves both telescoping and misreporting. Telescoping means accurately recalling when an event occurred. Previous studies on victimization (Dodge and Turner 1971; Sparks, Glenn, and Dodd 1977; Garofalo and Hindelang 1977) have observed some forward telescoping, with about 20 percent of the respondents reporting victimizations that had occurred prior to the period under study. The reverse process, backward telescoping, was noted at about the same rate in the Sparks study. As Skogan notes (1981:18), however, "While telescoping can be both forward and backward in time, the net effect of these two forces is strongly in the forward direction (Schneider, 1977). There is a significant tendency for respondents to 'move' events around in time, falsely describing them as being more recent than they actually were." Such memory distortions can produce either an inflation or a deflation in the actual number of cases reported in any given time period.

The issue of accurate time recall was examined in the San Jose record-check study by interviewing crime victims initially selected from police records (Turner 1972). The percentage of correctly recalled events (as having occurred within the past twelve months) varied by type of offense from a high of 90 percent for burglary to 48 percent for assault. About two-thirds of the rape victims in the sample correctly recalled their victimization as occurring within the past year.

Misreporting beyond just the temporal location of the incident may also seriously affect the validity of victimization reports. In a study comparing police and interview data on a variety of incident attributes, Schneider (1977) noted discrepancies on several features, such as the race of the offender, the victim-offender relationship, and the seriousness of the incident. These points of disagreement were not consistently related to length of recall. Schneider notes in conclusion that it is impossible to place responsibility for these inconsistencies solely on the survey or the police reports. Just as respondents may forget or misdescribe incidents, the police may not record certain reports as crime events or may systematically downgrade crimes in order to reduce the overall crime index.

Despite what appears to be a fair amount of research on the validity of victim reports, we still lack reliable, comprehensive data on the accuracy of victim reporting. Almost all information about the validity of rape reports comes from police record checks. Such checks tend to assume that police data are an appropriate, reliable source for assessing the veracity of victim reports. Yet as noted in the Schneider study (1977), police records are subject to error, change, and distortion just as are victims' memories.

More important, however, record checks provide information on only reported crimes, which according to the victimization surveys represent only about 50 percent of all serious crimes. Since it does not appear that any other kind of record-check validation has occurred (Skogan 1981), we are still in the position of knowing little about the validity of victim reports that are not part of police records.

Despite the limited state of our knowledge, the previous research coupled with our own understanding of the SAP data lead us to certain conclusions about their validity. First, the likelihood of telescoping introducing major error in the sexual-assault data is small. The reference period (the previous calendar year) was bounded by calling the respondents' attention to a significant event that occurred at both the beginning and end of the period. In addition, since the majority of the interviews were conducted in January and February of each year, there was very little lag time between the interview and the reference period. There was a small problem with the reporting of assaults that occurred in January or February just prior to the interview; once or twice these assaults were reported as occurring in the previous year. The month and year of the assault as reported in the sexual-assault section, however, usually allowed us to locate these assaults in the correct time period.

Nonreporting, whether purposive or unintentional, is probably the more-serious threat to the validity of the self-report sexual-assault data. Research indicates that for serious personal crimes such as sexual assault, a fair amount of underreporting occurs. When the assaults involve known or related assailants, the underreporting may increase dramatically. For the sexual-assault data, this suggests that the level of underreporting may be quite high because the majority of reported assaults among the youth population involve dates or acquaintances. Although the number of females who self-identified as victims and then refused to answer the sexual-assault questions was quite small, it is impossible to know how many victims failed to reveal their sexual-assault experience altogether.

Although the issue of exaggeration or overreporting was not examined in previous victimization studies, this may be a major problem in the sexual-assault data. Approximately 75 percent of the victims in each year responded to the item with the broadest wording—the date-rape item. As described by the victims, most of these experiences did not involve much, if any, physical force, and less than half were completed assaults. Since we do not know exactly what sexual activity occurred, we suspect that the date-rape item may have solicited reports of unpleasant, even pressured sexual experiences that nonetheless did not involve forced contact with the sexual parts of the body. Thus it is possible that some proportion of the sexual-assault reports are trivial and would not be considered legitimate sexual assaults.

How much of this overreporting is balanced by underreporting is difficult to estimate. The findings regarding both occurrences coupled with the fact that most victims responded to the date-rape item lead us to speculate that the problem of overreporting is likely to be the more severe for the victim data. Thus when formal estimates of the incidence and prevalence of sexual assault are presented (see chapter 3), the more-accurate estimates probably lie in the lower end of the .95 confidence intervals.

Offender Reports

The issues of nonresponse and inaccurate recall are as relevant for offender reports as they are for victim reports. In an effort to validate self-reports of delinquent behavior (including those of sexual assault), the NYS gathered police arrest data and compared respondents' official arrest records with their self-reported delinquent offenses in the same year. Subjects failing to report an offense similar to that for which an arrest was shown could be judged to have falsified the self-reported delinquency. This assumes, however, that police data are error free; they are not. As Elliott and his colleagues have noted (1983:33), "A person may have an arrest record for an offense s/he was suspected of but did not in fact commit; the police knowledge and description of an event may be limited, resulting in a less serious or different charge than reported by an offender; or clerical errors may lead to an incorrect assignment of an arrest record to a participant in the study." Although we do not expect these errors to be frequent, mismatches between police and self-report data should not automatically be treated as evidence of the invalidity of the latter.

This matching procedure indicates that over one out of five male youth with an arrest record may have concealed part of their involvement in delinquent behavior.[5] The amount of underreporting was more pronounced among black males (in comparison to white males) and was more prevalent for serious (Uniform Crime Report index offenses) than nonserious offenses. Whether this rate of underreporting may be generalized to the full NYS sample is not known since it is based on a subsample (youth with arrests) that may or may not be representative of the total sample. It is the case, however, that this level of underreporting for arrested youth is comparable to that observed by other researchers employing police record checks (Hindelang, Hirschi, and Weis 1981; Elliott and Voss 1974; Gold 1966). Although we believe that some portion of this underreporting probably represents errors in police records or our matching procedures rather than deliberate concealment or inaccurate recall on the part of respondents, it is clear that underreporting is a source of error in self-reported delinquency measures.

To address the question of overreporting, we examined the distribution of responses on the three sexual-assault items. Across the three years, 56 percent of the offenders reponded to the date-rape item, 34 percent responded to the item "had sexual relations with someone against their will," and 10 percent entered the sample by indicating that they had threatened or physically harmed someone for sex. In each year, from 47 percent to 61 percent of the sexual-assault offenders responded to the date-rape item. A review of the descriptions of these incidents suggests that a number of them reflect the classic dating scenario where the male presses the female for sex. Most of these incidents did not involve more than verbal pressure, and a high proportion were unsuccessful attempts according to the offender reports.

These findings suggest that some of the incidents reported under the date-rape item might not be considered legitimate sexual assaults. We suspect that some exaggeration or embellishment has occurred, though the exact level is impossible to determine. From our own knowledge of the data, however, we believe the problem of underreporting to be the more-serious source of error, for several reasons. First, we believe there is more social stigma associated with reporting the commission of a sexual assault than with other crimes, a situation that should depress the number of reported sexual assaults. Second, the results of the police record check suggest a moderate amount of underreporting and that it is more pronounced for serious crimes, such as rape and sexual assault. Finally, the proportion of males who initially reported a sexual assault and then deselected themselves or refused to answer any further questions is almost double that for the female victims. This differential may be attributed to males who reported legitimate sexual assaults and then downplayed the seriousness of the event once they realized they were going to be questioned about it. For these reasons, we believe that underreporting is the more-serious source of error in the offender data. Thus when the formal estimates of the prevalence and incidence of sexual assault are presented (in chapter 7), the upper ends of the .95 confidence intervals probably contain the more accurate estimates.

There is likely to be a fair amount of error in both the victim and offender data. It is exceedingly difficult to measure accurately illegal and socially stigmatizing behavior such as sexual assault. When an attempted seduction becomes a sexual assault is open to interpretation, and males and females are likely to differ in their judgment of this. This issue is especially ambiguous when the setting is a date and the two participants are acquainted. Furthermore, we believe there is a natural tendency for those who feel victimized to justify themselves by maximizing their description of the assault. Similarly offenders are likely to downplay the seriousness of an assault by underestimating the coercion and force they used.

Nonetheless these are problems that plague all sexual-assault research, some efforts more than others. The SAP attempted to address as many of these concerns as possible and to minimize the impact they could have on the data. Although we are not unaware of the error in our estimates, there is good reason to believe that these self-report data provide substantially more-accurate estimates of the incidence and prevalence of sexual assault than do official data.

The final issue of concern regarding the reliability and validity of these data relates to the use of the self-report technique. Although the accuracy of data generated using a voluntary reporting method, especially for illegal or sensitive, personal behaviors, has often been questioned, there is good evidence to suggest that such techniques produce reasonably reliable results. In a study of induced abortions (Gebhard et al. 1958), it was demonstrated through independent interviewers that there was 95 percent agreement between husbands and wives as to the number and timing of induced abortions even though many were illegal. A large body of research on self-report delinquency measures has assessed their validity and reliability with such techniques as lie scales and social-desirability scales (Hardt and Bodine 1965), known-group differences (Nye and Short 1957; Reiss and Rhodes 1959; Voss 1963), and a standard test-retest format (Clark and Tifft 1966; Clark and Wenninger 1962; Dentler and Monroe 1961). The general results of these tests suggest that self-report measures produce accurate, valid data. More important, recent work by Hardt and Peterson-Hardt (1977), Hindelang, Hirschi, and Weis (1981), and Huizinga and Elliott (1983) on the reliability and validity of self-report delinquency measures reconfirms the earlier findings. The general consensus from this contemporary research is that the self-report technique is basically a valid and reliable procedure for measuring delinquency and other sensitive, personal behavior.

The use of the self-report procedure is critical to a study of sexual assault given the general assumption (at least partly supported by research) that from a quarter to a half or more of all sexual-assault victims never report to the authorities (Feldman-Summers 1976; Flanagan, van Alstyne, and Gottfredson 1982). Even taking the lower figure, police statistics always seriously underestimate the incidence of sexual assault. Furthermore, it is unlikely that reported cases of sexual assault are representative of all cases, and hence the distribution of cases based on official data is likely to be biased. Although self-report sexual-assault data are certainly not free from error or bias, their potential for providing reasonable estimates of the incidence, prevalence, and distribution of sexual assault is much greater than that of official statistics.

Description of the Data Base

Three general groups of variables were used in the analyses: sociodemographic variables, general attitudinal and behavioral scales, and data specific to the sexual-assault reported.

Sociodemographic Variables

Four standard sociodemographic variables are used throughout the analyses: age, race, social class, and place of residence.[6] Age is a continuous variable, with the possible ages ranging from eleven to twenty-one. Age is determined by birthdate. All race analyses are comparisons of whites and blacks only. Other racial groups have been excluded because the sample sizes were too small for reliable estimates.

The social-class measure is the Hollingshead two-factor index (Hollingshead and Redlich 1958) as applied to the principal wage earner in each youth's family. Hollingshead classes I and II, involving primarily professional managerial occupations with college-level educations, are collapsed to make the middle-class category. Hollingshead class III, consisting primarily of owners of small businesses, clerical workers, and persons in sales and skilled manual occupations with high school or some college completed, constitutes the working-class category. The lower-class category is composed of classes IV and V, primarily semiskilled persons and those in unskilled manual occupations with high school or lower levels of education.

The place- of-residence classification is based on U.S. Census descriptions of the cities, towns, and areas where respondents lived. Urban areas in this classification are central cities of a Standard Metropolitan Statistical Area (SMSA) or an urbanized area with a population of 100,000 or more.

Suburban areas are central cities of an urbanized area with a population less than 100,000 or any part of a SMSA not previously classified as urban, or any community with a population of 25,000 or more. Rural areas are cities or places not included in a SMSA or part of a central city in an urbanized area with a population less than 25,000. During the study, respondents who moved were assigned a new place-of-residence score.

General Attitudinal and Behavioral Scales

A number of behavioral and attitudinal scales were used in the analyses. These were defined by the theoretical model for the offenders and the conceptual work related to predicting vulnerability for the victims. Brief descriptions of these scales along with their reliabilities and homogeneity ratios are provided in appendixes A and B. As appendix B shows, most of the scales demonstrate adequate psychometric properties.

Specific Sexual-Assault Items

The sexual-assault portion of the NYS interview schedule contained a separate set of questions for the victims and the offenders. The victim questions covered basic descriptive data about the assault such as the time of the year; place of the assault; number, age, and sex of offender(s); relationship of the victim to the offender(s); type of force and pressure experienced; resistance offered; whether the assault was reported to the police; perception of factors that precipitated the assault, and so on. In addition, data were gathered on the reactions of friends, parents, and others to the assault, any changes in the behavior of the victim as a consequence of the assault, and efforts by the victim to deal with the assault by seeking help or counseling. Finally, the victim's own reactions to the assault within a week of the event and at the time of the interview were solicited.

The offender set contained the same basic descriptive data about the assault as the victim set: time of year; location; number, age, and sex of victim(s); relationship to victim(s); amount of force and pressure used; and so on. In addition, the offenders were asked about planning the assault and whether they had been drinking or taking drugs prior to the assault. Finally, they were queried about their own reactions to the assault, as well as the reactions of their friends who knew about it. A complete list of the victim and offender questions included in the sexual-assault interview appears in appendix C.

Theoretically the recall period from the time of the sexual assault to the interview ranged from one to twelve months. In reality, the longest recall period was typically only six months because three-quarters of the sexual assaults (reported by both victims and offenders) had occurred in the last six months of each year.

General Analytical Approach

Four general levels of data analysis were undertaken. First, incidence and prevalence estimates were calculated separately for each of the three years 1978 through 1980. These estimates were calculated by race, social class, age, and place of residence for the female victims and male offenders. These figures provide baseline data on the frequency, proportion of cases, and distribution of sexual assault among adolescents in the United States. Second, descriptive data were compiled on the victims, offenders, the nature of the assault, and the initial and over-time effects on the victims of being sexually assaulted. These data are used to generate descriptive profiles of both adolescent victims and offenders, as well as to assess the personal and situational factors associated with brief or prolonged reactions to an assault.

The third set of analyses are composed of annual (1978 through 1980) t-tests between the victims and randomly generated control groups and the offenders and similarly constructed control groups on a broad range of variables. Significant differences between the groups are noted, as well as any trends or patterns in these differences. It is anticipated that the results from these analyses may help to define victim vulnerability and distinguish adolescent sexual-assault offenders from their nonoffending peers. Finally, a series of discriminant analyses were undertaken to test the predictive capacity of the offender theoretical model.

Notes

1. In general when we refer to the adolescent period, we are talking about the age range thirteen through nineteen; however, in the first two years of the NYS, eleven and twelve year olds are included and in the final two years, twenty- and twenty-one-year-old youth are included.

2. We are using the phrase *date rape* to cover the range of forced sexual behavior that may occur in the context of a date.

3. These 172 interviews represent only 135 females; several victims reported in more than one year.

4. These 68 interviews represent only 51 males; several offenders reported in more than one year.

Research Methods and Procedures

5. Although we wanted to conduct this match just with male sexual-assault offenders, the number who had arrests for offenses we could match with self-report delinquency items was too small to draw any reliable conclusions about the group.

6. Sex is not a relevant variable because the analyses focus on female victims and male offenders.

**Part II
The Adolescent Victim**

3
The Nature and Extent of Sexual Assault among Adolescent Females, 1978–1980

Prevalence and Incidence Estimates

One advantage of a probability sample is that sample means and proportions may be generalized to the full population with a known degree of accuracy. With the sexual-assault sample, this means that the annual prevalence and incidence of sexual assault may be estimated for the female adolescent population aged thirteen through nineteen in 1978, fourteen through twenty in 1979, and fifteen through twenty-one in 1980. References in this chapter to the female adolescent population are always in the context of these age groups.

In this book, prevalence figures for sexual-assault victims indicate the proportion of females who were sexually assaulted one or more times within a specific year. The average frequency of sexual assaults per female adolescent for each year is represented by the incidence figures.

Since there were several sexual-assault items that a victim could respond to, it is possible that the same event was reported more than once. To ensure that the incidence figures do not contain any replications, a sorting procedure was used during the interview to obtain a nonredundant count of the number of independent sexual assaults experienced during a year period. This number was used in the incidence calculations rather than the actual frequencies reported for each sexual-assault item.

One additional adjustment was made to the sexual-assault figures: all reports from potential victims who later deselected were not included in either the incidence or the prevalence estimates. Hence, to the best of our knowledge, the incidence and prevalence estimates represent only legitimate, independent cases of sexual assault reported in 1978, 1979, and 1980.

Table 3–1 displays estimates of the prevalence of sexual assault among female youth for the years 1978 through 1980.[1] These estimates are presented as the proportion of females reporting one or more sexual assaults in each of the three years. In addition, the .95 confidence interval for each proportion is presented. These data are provided for all females and then by age, social class, race, and place of residence.

The figures in table 3–1 indicate that for each of the years covered, from 7 to 9 percent of the female adolescent population in the appropriate age

Table 3-1
Proportion of Female Youth Reporting One or More Sexual Assaults by Age, Social Class, Race, and Place of Residence, 1978–1980

		1978			1979			1980	
	N	Proportion	.95 Confidence Interval	N	Proportion	.95 Confidence Interval	N	Proportion	.95 Confidence Interval
Total female sample	763	.084	.062–.106	738	.085	.065–.106	711	.068	.045–.090
Ages by year									
1978 / 1979 / 1980									
13 / 14 / 15	117	.026*	.000–.055	111	.072	.013–.132	111	.036	.000–.082
14 / 15 / 16	126	.079	.044–.115	122	.082	.038–.126	119	.067	.026–.109
15 / 16 / 17	125	.096	.038–.154	126	.087	.038–.136	123	.073	.016–.131
16 / 17 / 18	102	.069	.018–.119	99	.111	.051–.171	95	.095	.027–.163
17 / 18 / 19	108	.120	.042–.199	104	.096	.046–.146	98	.051	.007–.096
18 / 19 / 20	100	.060	.013–.107	96	.073	.020–.125	89	.067	.014–.121
19 / 20 / 21	85	.153*	.084–.222	80	.075	.016–.134	76	.092	.036–.148
Social class									
Middle	192	.078	.037–.119	184	.092	.051–.134	171	.053	.018–.088
Working	228	.079	.039–.119	222	.099	.064–1.35	223	.090	.057–.122
Lower	306	.092	.058–.125	298	.074	.038–.110	285	.067	.030–.103
Race									
White	616	.076	.058–.094	595	.082	.061–.103	576	.064	.041–.087
Black	103	.097	.028–.166	99	.111	.039–.183	94	.064	.000–.135
Place of residence									
Urban	196	.077	.029–.124	196	.107*	.062–.150	187	.102*	.055–.148
Suburban	348	.095	.061–.129	339	.091	.057–.125	319	.063	.031–.094
Rural	219	.073	.037–.109	203	.054*	.027–.081	203	.044*	.013–.076

Notes: Several of the subgroup sample sizes do not add to the total sample N due to missing data or, in the case of race, the absence of the other minority group cases from this table.

Across the three years, the average design effect for the total sample and all subgroups is 1.02.

*Differences significant at $p \leq .05$ for groups so marked.

ranges experienced one or more sexual assaults. Taking into account the confidence intervals and national estimates of the adolescent female population, the actual number of youthful female victims in any one year could be as low as 600,000 or as high as 1.5 million. For all females, the rate of sexual assault is fairly constant across the three years.[2]

With the exception that the youngest age groups in each year report the smallest proportionate involvement in sexual assault, the age data show no consistent age-related patterns. The statistical comparisons between the youngest and oldest groups in each year produced a significant difference only in 1978.[3] These findings do not indicate that older females are consistently more vulnerable to sexual assault than their younger counterparts.

Within years, no significant differences in prevalence of sexual assault are noted by either social class or race. Across the three years surveyed, no one class or racial group consistently shows the highest or lowest prevalence score. These data do not support the commonly held belief that black and lower-class females are more vulnerable to sexual assault than their white middle- and working-class peers.

The location of one's residence, however, does seem to affect the sexual-assault prevalence estimates. In two of the three years surveyed, significant differences in the proportion of females reporting a sexual assault were noted between the urban and rural categories. In both 1979 and 1980, the proportion of urban females reporting a sexual assault was at least twice that of rural females. Although the urban-rural difference was not significant in 1978, the direction was consistent with the other two years, suggesting that urban females are more vulnerable to sexual assault than are their rural peers.

In conjunction with the prevalence estimates, some understanding of the frequency of occurrence of sexual assault is also important. Table 3–2 presents the incidence of sexual assault for adolescent females for the years 1978 through 1980 using the same set of demographic variables as with the prevalence estimates. These data reflect the average annual frequency of sexual assault for female adolescents, ages thirteen to nineteen in 1978, fourteen to twenty in 1979, and fifteen to twenty-one in 1980. The mean scores show that the incidence of sexual assault rose from 1978 to 1979 and then tapered off in 1980. Using the confidence intervals, these averages translate into from 1.3 million to 2.6 million sexual assaults in 1978 and from 1 million to 5.7 million sexual assaults in 1979.

With one exception, none of the within-year comparisons by race, social class, age, or place of residence produce any significant differences. The exception is the comparison between the lowest age group and the highest in 1978. The average frequency of sexual assault for the nineteen year olds is

Table 3-2
Average Number of Sexual Assaults per Female by Age, Social Class, Race, and Place of Residence, 1978-1980

	1978			1979			1980		
	N	Mean	.95 Confidence Interval	N	Mean	.95 Confidence Interval	N	Mean	.95 Confidence Interval
Total female sample	763	0.143	0.095–0.191	738	0.238	0.071–0.406	711	0.193	0.079–0.306
Ages by year									
1978 / 1979 / 1980									
13 / 14 / 15	117	0.026*	0.000–0.055	111	0.108	0.000–0.230	111	0.054	0.000–0.123
14 / 15 / 16	126	0.135	0.051–0.219	122	0.115	0.040–0.190	119	0.387	0.000–1.000
15 / 16 / 17	125	0.224	0.042–0.406	126	0.516	0.000–1.296	123	0.236	0.011–0.461
16 / 17 / 18	102	0.108	0.012–0.204	99	0.222	0.070–0.375	95	0.242	0.000–0.495
17 / 18 / 19	108	0.213	0.053–0.373	104	0.356	0.110–0.601	98	0.153	0.000–0.350
18 / 19 / 20	100	0.060	0.013–0.107	96	0.177	0.010–0.344	89	0.090	0.015–0.165
19 / 20 / 21	85	0.247*	0.114–0.380	80	0.113	0.016–0.209	76	0.132	0.065–0.198
Social class									
Middle	192	0.104	0.046–0.163	184	0.234	0.117–0.351	171	0.076	0.020–0.132
Working	228	0.189	0.059–0.318	222	0.387	0.000–0.852	223	0.336	0.043–0.630
Lower	306	0.134	0.083–0.185	298	0.121	0.047–0.195	285	0.172	0.052–0.292
Race									
White	616	0.136	0.086–0.186	595	0.257	0.051–0.463	576	0.179	0.035–0.322
Black	103	0.126	0.034–0.219	99	0.141	0.038–0.244	94	0.255	0.000–0.577
Place of residence									
Urban	196	0.122	0.046–0.199	196	0.153	0.085–0.221	187	0.209	0.037–0.380
Suburban	348	0.132	0.079–0.186	339	0.236	0.131–0.341	319	0.129	0.054–0.203
Rural	219	0.178	0.058–0.298	203	0.325	0.000–0.825	203	0.281	0.000–0.649

Notes: Several of the subgroup sample sizes do not add to the total sample N due to missing data or, in the case of race, the absence of the other minority group cases from this table.

Across the three years, the average design effect for the total sample and all subgroups is 1.02.

*Differences significant at $p \leq .05$ for groups so marked.

eight times what it is for the thirteen year olds in this year. This appears to be an isolated finding, however; no consistent age patterns emerge in the subsequent two years of data.

Despite the lack of significant differences, there are some interesting patterns in the incidence data. For example, it appears that on the average, working-class females experience more sexual assaults than their middle- or lower-class counterparts. The working- to middle-class incidence ratios range from a low of two to one to a high of nearly five to one, while the working- to lower-class ratios range from three to two to three to one. When the place-of-residence data are inspected, it is somewhat surprising to discover that the highest incidence scores are consistently found in the rural group. Since this group has the lowest proportionate involvement in sexual assault (see table 3–1), the incidence and prevalence data together indicate that a fairly small number of rural females reported a relatively large number of sexual assaults.

In summary, the prevalence and incidence estimates indicate that from 1978 through 1980, nearly 10 percent of the female youth population experienced at least one sexual assault annually, and that the average annual frequency of sexual assaults over this period was approximately 0.19. No consistent, significant differences were observed by age, social class, or race; however, the proportion of urban females experiencing a sexual assault was significantly higher than it was for rural females. As this panel of female youth matured from thirteen to nineteen years of age in 1978 to fifteen to twenty-one in 1980, the incidence and prevalence of sexual assault were not affected in any uniform way. Although we did not conduct statistical tests to assess age differences controlling for cohort effects, an examination of tables 3–1 and 3–2 suggests that the prevalence and incidence of sexual assault do not increase with age.

Given the level and type of error in these prevalence and incidence estimates, we believe that the lower ends of the .95 confidence intervals probably contain the more-accurate estimates. The secondary nature of the research precluded the use of some procedures and the asking of certain questions that could have improved the precision of the estimates. It is important that these estimates be interpreted within the context in which they were generated.

Comparisons with Uniform Crime Reports and the National Crime Survey

The SAP data may stand by themselves, but it is difficult to interpret them in a vacuum. Comparable or similar data sources are needed as benchmarks against which to compare and contrast the SAP findings. The two most-logical data sets for this purpose are the Uniform Crime Reports (UCR) and the National Crime Survey (NCS). The former provide annual statistics on crime in the United States as measured by arrests and offenses that come to the attention of the law-enforcement community. For our purposes, these data offer information on the number of forcible rapes reported annually to the police. The second data source, the NCS, reports annual victimization data generated from a continuing survey of a representative sample of households across the United States, containing about 135,000 individuals. These are self-report data and reflect individual (as well as household) reports of all types of victimization, including forcible rape.

Although neither of these data sets is directly comparable to the SAP data, to our knowledge they are the only other national data available on rape and sexual assault. Hence, the UCR and NCS appear to be the only logical bases for comparison. Careful attention to the differences and similarities among these three data sources will permit an interpretation of the SAP findings without presenting misleading or distorted conclusions. Several differences need to be addressed before beginning any comparisons.

Probably the most-obvious difference among the three data sets is that two (the SAP and NCS) use self-reports of victimization derived under survey-research methods; the third (the UCR) reflects crimes known (generally reported) to the police or other law-enforcement agencies. Although all three data sets have a problem with underreporting, the error from this source is likely to be greatest in the UCR. Victimization research has indicated consistently that only about half of the forcible rapes (or attempts) are ever reported to the police (Flanagan, van Alstyne, and Gottfredson 1982: figure 3.1). Furthermore, of those rapes reported, some proportion are judged unfounded by the police and never become part of the UCR statistics on rape. Thus for purposes of determining incidence (prevalence cannot be derived from the UCR because of the way the data are collected), the UCR are clearly the most conservative.

Another important distinction among the three data sets is the definition of rape and sexual assault that is employed. Both the UCR and NCS record incidents of forcible rape or attempts at such. No other types of sexual assault are measured. The SAP uses a much broader definition, which encompasses forcible rape but also a variety of other forced sexual behaviors, all of which do not constitute rape. Consequently we would anticipate that the incidence derived from the SAP figures would be larger than that from the NCS and substantially larger than that from the UCR.

While it is possible to match the ages of the victims from the NCS and SAP data sets, the UCR do not classify their data by age of victim; hence we can examine the figures only for all rape victims. The effect of this is to

Sexual Assault among Females   31

inflate the UCR data when they are being compared with only adolescent data from the other data sources.

Given these incompatibilities, it may seem useless and inappropriate to attempt to relate the three data sets. The UCR and NCS, and especially the former, however, have been the basis of knowledge of the incidence and distribution of rape for some time. If we are to refine and expand our knowledge base, we must continually reassess the existing data in the light of new data. This is not to say that one data set or another will or should be judged superior or correct but only that we may come to understand the differences and distinct applications among the three.

Table 3-3 displays the rates of reported rape or sexual assault per 1,000 females derived from the NCS, SAP, and UCR data sets for the years 1978 through 1980.[4] For a better comparison with the forcible-rape data from the UCR and NCS, the SAP reports involving violent force and/or a weapon have been presented separately. Although all of these cases might not qualify as forcible rapes, they probably represent the most-serious sexual assaults reported.

As expected, the lowest rate is derived from the UCR data and the highest from the total count of all sexual assaults drawn from the SAP. The sizable difference between the NCS and UCR (even without including adult

Table 3-3
Rape and Sexual-Assault Rates for Females, per 1,000 Population

Data Source	1978	1979	1980
Uniform Crime Reports (all ages)	0.31	0.34	0.36
National Crime Survey (ages 12-19)	3.50	4.19	[a]
Sexual Assault Project (ages 13-21) Sexual assaults involving physical violence and/or a weapon	9.17	6.78	12.66
All sexual assaults[b]	95.00	71.00	79.00

Sources: *Uniform Crime Reports*, 1978, 1979, and 1980: pp. 14, 13, 14, respectively. *Criminal Victimization in the United States*, 1978, 1979: table 5.

Notes: The UCR and NCS count forcible rape and attempts only. Forcible rape is defined as the carnal knowledge of a female forcibly and against her will. Assaults or attempts to commit rape by force or threat of force are also included but not statutory rape (without force) and other sex offenses. The SAP counts all forced sexual acts (including attempts) involving contact between the victims' and offenders' sexual parts, against the will of the victim.

Because forcible rape and violent sexual assault are relatively rare, the NCS estimates and those from the SAP based on physically violent sexual assaults are subject to a fair amount of sampling error. Although this error limits the precision of these estimates, they are still the best estimates available.

[a]The 1980 NCS data were not available.
[b]In an attempt to adjust for overreporting, these estimates reflect the lower end of the .95 confidence interval.

females in the NCS data) suggests how much the official police reports underestimate the incidence of forcible rape. The NCS rate is more than ten times that of the UCR even without considering the age differences. Thus conclusions drawn from UCR data are likely to underestimate vastly the amount of forcible rape occurring in the female population.

More important from our perspective is the fact that even the NCS, using a self-report technique similar to that of the SAP, appears to be capturing only a small portion of the total amount of forced sexual behavior occurring among the female adolescent population. Given the broader definition of sexual assault employed by the SAP, the large differential between the NCS rate of forcible rape and that for all sexual assaults derived from the SAP is not surprising. However, even with the more-appropriate comparison between forcible rape and violent sexual assaults, there is still a sizable difference between the two rates. The rate of serious, violent sexual assaults derived from the SAP is well over two times the NCS rate in 1978 and two-thirds again as large as the NCS rate in 1979. The sizable increase in the SAP rate of these physically violent assaults in 1980 suggests that the differential between the NCS and the SAP would be substantial in this year as well.

Since both of these data sources employ the self-report technique and cover approximately the same age range, the discrepancy in rates must be explained by other factors. We suspect that at least part of it is due to the different definitions of the phenomena of interest. The SAP data even when restricted to the cases most akin to forcible rape are not as precisely focused on this type of behavior as are the NCS data. Part of the difference in rates surely lies here.

We believe that a large part of the differential may be attributable to the method by which the data were obtained. The NCS data are gathered for an entire household with all members twelve years of age and older eligible to participate. Thus all members of a household above a certain age are potential respondents and become aware that participation beyond an initial screening indicates some type of victimization. Inasmuch as our findings indicate that over three-quarters of the adolescent victims did not tell their parents about their assault, we suspect that a similar proportion would not report on a survey in which their parents were involved.

In contrast, the SAP interviewed only adolescents, and the interview was focused on a wide variety of issues, attitudes, and behaviors, only one of which was victimization. The possibility of reporting a sexual assault in private to an SAP interviewer and still keeping this incident secret from one's parents is substantially higher than on the NCS. Although other sources of error and bias surely affect the two rates as well, the different procedures for gathering victimization reports may account for a substantial portion of the discrepancy in the rates of forcible rape and violent sexual assault.

In summary, these general comparisons across data sources indicate that the conclusions we draw about the incidence of rape and sexual assault will vary considerably depending on the data source. Of the three sources examined, the UCR are the most limited for estimations of incidence. Reports of forcible rape to the police appear to represent less than half of these events in the population. Given the size and quality of the sample and the sophisticated research methodology, the NCS data probably provide the best total estimates of the actual incidence of forcible rape. We believe, however, that the NCS data may seriously underestimate the rate of forcible rape among adolescents. Furthermore, these data reflect only one type of sexual assault.

To the best of our knowledge, the SAP data are the only source for national estimates of the incidence and prevalence of all forced sexual behavior experienced by adolescents. Inasmuch as sexual assault is a broader category of behavior than forcible rape, one would expect the SAP estimates to be larger than those derived from the NCS, as they are. The accuracy of these estimates, however, is dependent on the reliability and validity of the self-report data, the representiveness of the sample, and the amount of sampling error. We feel confident about the quality of the sample, but voluntary reporting of a stressful and socially stigmatizing experience such as a sexual assault always carries with it the possibility of underreporting and purposive concealment. We also have to acknowledge that overreporting and exaggeration may inflate the estimates of all sexual assault. The precise effect of these factors on the estimates is impossible to calculate since, depending on the direction, magnitude, and distribution of each type of error, they could balance each other out or produce underestimates or overestimates. Assuming that the largest source of error is likely to be from overreporting (at least regarding the nonviolent events), the more-realistic estimates of incidence probably are located in the lower segments of the .95 confidence intervals.

Comparison of Victim Profiles

Profiles of rape victims have been developed from a variety of sources, including police records, emergency-room files, treatment-center records, and population surveys. Although most of these sources are restricted to reported or known rape victims and therefore cannot be considered representative, they nonetheless have been used to typify rape victims (see Katz and Mazur 1979:33–44 for a discussion of the demographic characteristics of rape victims and a list of sources for these data). For our purposes, the general profile derived from these data will be presented only to provide a background against which to compare the profile of adolescent victims generated from the NCS and SAP.[5]

The popular profile depicts the rape victim as a young (predominately teenage and young adult) black, lower-class, unmarried female residing in an urban area. A recent study based on a large number of rape victims drawn from hospital records generally confirms this demographic profile (McCahill, Meyer, and Fischman 1979).

The most-recent NCS data confirm part of this profile and refute other parts of it. The rate of forcible rape is substantially higher for adolescents and young adults than all other age groups, with the sixteen- to nineteen-year-old females reporting the highest rate of all. The NCS data also show that as a group, black females have a higher rate than white females; however, in two of the three years under examination, this race differential reverses itself when we restrict the comparison just to adolescents. In 1977 and 1979, the rate of forcible rape for white females, ages twelve to fifteen and sixteen to nineteen, was higher than that of the same-age black females (see Flanagan, Hindelang, and Gottfredson 1980 and Flanagan, van Alstyne, and Gottfredson 1982:table 3.11). Even the twenty- to twenty-four-year-old age group evidences a higher rate of forcible rape for whites than for blacks, at least in 1979. Among adolescents, the NCS data do not appear to support the image of the typical rape victim as black.

With regard to marital status and social class, the NCS data reinforce the standard rape-victim profile. Unmarried and divorced (or separated) females as well as those from households with incomes below $7,500 have higher rates of forcible rape than married, higher-income females. Since these data are not cross-classified by both sex and age, we cannot determine whether these factors would differentiate female adolescent victims in the same way they do all female victims. Although the marital-status factor is probably meaningless for adolescents since such a large proportion of them are unmarried, the social-class factor is certainly relevant.

As might be expected, the NCS data show a relationship between risk of rape and size of place of residence. The highest rates of forcible rape are in central cities of metropolitan areas; the lowest are in nonmetropolitan areas. The size of the rate generally increases with the population of the central city, but there are exceptions. Again the presentation of the data do not permit assessing the relevance of this factor for just adolescent rape victims.

For all women, the NCS data tend to support the typical profile of rape victims as young, black, unmarried women from the lower class who are residing in an urban area. With regard to race, however, this image appears to be less appropriate for female adolescent victims. The risk of forcible rape is higher for white teenagers than black, especially in the youngest age group. For twelve- to fifteen-year-old white adolescents in 1979, the rate of forcible rape is almost double that of their black peers. Among female teenagers, the NCS data clearly indicate that the typical rape victim is white. Whether other aspects of the rape-victim profile would be altered for youthful rape victims if the appropriate data were available (that is, data on social class, place of residence, and marital-status cross-classified by sex and age) is open to question. Furthermore, the effect of underreporting on the distribution of rape victims is difficult to assess. Certainly these issues plus the atypical race finding for teenage victims lead us to question the appropriateness of the general NCS rape-victim profile for adolescent victims of rape.

Analyses of both the prevalence and incidence data from the SAP evidence no significant race or social-class differences among sexual-assault victims. Thus in terms of both the proportion of females involved and the number of incidents, no substantial racial or socioeconomic disparities were noted. The data do show, however, that the proportion of urban females reporting a sexual assault was significantly higher than the proportion of rural females. All of the SAP findings taken together suggest that both the prevalence and incidence of sexual assault are fairly evenly distributed by race and social class but not by place of residence (at least regarding prevalence).

When we examine the demographic characteristics of those SAP victims who reported that a weapon and/or physical violence were used against them, the more-typical profile emerges. These youthful victims of violent sexual assaults are predominately black (or minority), lower-class, urban females. This distribution of sociodemographic features is present in all three years analyzed.

Across the data sets reviewed, it appears generally that victims of forcible rape and physically violent sexual assaults are disproportionately black, lower-class, urban females. The race reversal in the NCS data showing white adolescents more at risk than blacks is an exception; however, when adolescent victims of all types of sexual assault are analyzed demographically, we find no race or social-class differences, although urban females are more at risk.

In review, it appears that the profile one draws of a teenage rape or sexual-assault victim is somewhat dependent on the data source. More important, however, the breadth or narrowness of the definition of rape or sexual assault may dramatically affect the victim profile achieved. While adolescent females of all racial and social-class groups appear equally at risk of a sexual assault generally, vulnerability to a forcible rape or a violent sexual assault appears to be greatest among black and lower-class teenagers. City dwellers face a higher risk of all types of forced sexual behavior.

Probability of Being Sexually Assaulted

While the annual probability of being sexually assaulted at least once has already been presented, the SAP data also lend themselves to predicting the likelihood of incurring another assault within a specified period of time. Three additional probability figures may be calculated to determine the chances of incurring another assault within the same year period as the first sexual assault,[6] the year immediately following the year of the initial assault, and a two-year period after the year of the first sexual assault. These figures may answer some questions about the risk of sexual assault and whether it changes after one has experienced an assault.

For 1978, 36 percent of those who were sexually assaulted at least once reported being assaulted two or more times in that year. The comparable figures in 1979 and 1980 were 43 percent and 44 percent, respectively. These figures indicate that well over one-third of those who reported an assault in each of these years experienced at least one more assault within the same year period. If these statistics are compared with the annual prevalence figures for the same years, one concludes that for a year period, the probability of being sexually assaulted increases dramatically once one has experienced an assault.

The effect of an assault in one year on the likelihood of another assault in the following year was also determined. Estimates for the years 1978 through 1979 and 1979 through 1980 were calculated to reflect the proportion of victims who report at least one assault in each of two consecutive years. Twenty-five percent of those who reported an assault in 1978 reported another assault in 1979; the equivalent figure for the 1979-1980 comparison was 32 percent. Once having been sexually assaulted, the risk of another assault in the following year increases three to four times over the annual probability figure for all female adolescents.

A final probability figure may be calculated for a two-year period after the year of the initial sexual assault. This figure is based on those who reported a sexual assault in 1978 and then reported at least one more assault in 1979 or 1980. More than one-third (37 percent) of those who had been sexually assaulted in 1978 indicated that they had been assaulted again in either 1979 or 1980 or in both years. Thus the risk of another assault within a two-year period is considerably higher than the annual prevalence of sexual assault; however, it is not that much higher than the probability of a second assault within the year following the first.

In summary, these results suggest that for that part of the female adolescent population that has been sexually assaulted, the risk of an assault in the future increases substantially over that for those who have not been assaulted.

Notes

1. Since sexual assault is relatively rare, at least in comparison to most other types of victimization, the number of sexual-assault cases in the

sample is rather small. Thus the sampling error may be large relative to the estimated proportions and means. As a result, it is better to focus on the confidence interval around each mean or proportion as it depicts the range in which the actual values are likely to fall.

2. We did not conduct any statistical comparisons of prevalence and incidence estimates across years because of the problem of controlling for age. With a panel design, the sample ages each year and thus differences between years may be attributed to age unless the age groups are identical. Since not all of the age groups are present in each year (for example, we have thirteen year olds only in 1978), we could conduct over time comparisons only with a reduced sample. Given this situation, coupled with the fact that many of the prevalence (and incidence) changes over time were relatively small (and therefore unlikely to be significant), we chose not to conduct any statistical comparisons between years.

3. Because of the number of age categories, we conducted statistical comparisons only between the youngest and oldest age groups in each year. We followed this procedure for both the prevalence and incidence estimates and for the offender data as well as the victim data.

4. Forcible rape and violent sexual assault are relatively rare. Hence the NCS data and those from the SAP based on violent sexual assaults are subject to a fair amount of sampling error, which limits the precision of these estimates.

5. The UCR do not collect and tabulate information on the personal characteristics of rape victims.

6. The first sexual assault refers to the initial one reported in the period 1978 through 1980. It is certainly possible that respondents could have been sexually assaulted prior to 1978, and hence an assault reported in that year would not have been their first assault.

4

The Sexual-Assault Experience from the Victim's Perspective

The sexual-assault descriptions in this chapter are a summation of 172 separate assaults reported for the period 1978 through 1980.[1] The findings from the three years are often cumulated rather than presented individually. The data lend themselves to summarization on several grounds. First, a standard set of questions was asked of all victims in each of the three years, and the interviews were conducted during the same time period in each year. Second, there are few substantial differences across the years on any of the major variables. Where they do appear, they are noted and discussed. In cases where victims reported more than one assault per year, they were asked to describe the most-recent event. This approach was selected because it was not possible to gather detailed information on all of the assaults reported and because we wanted a consistent point of reference for all of the assaults described. Although this approach may have improved the accuracy of the information reported because it entails the shortest recall period, it does not necessarily provide a representative description of all assaults experienced in the period 1978 through 1980.

Circumstances of a Sexual Assault

Approximately three-quarters of the assaults for the years 1978 through 1980 took place in one of three settings: a vehicle, the offender's home, or the victim's home. Across the three years, no one location was dominant, and in fact, each setting had the highest number of reports in one of the three years. The remaining 25 percent of the assaults occurred in a variety of locations, such as motel or hotel rooms, schools or other public buildings, and out of doors.

One additional piece of information is relevant here, even though it is available only for 1980. In the last survey, we asked whether the assault took place in the victim's neighborhood or the area in which she had lived for most of 1980. Almost two-thirds of the victims indicated that it had, yet only 23 percent had reported being assaulted in their homes. Clearly a number of assaults occur outside the victims' residences yet within the area they consider their neighborhood. This finding indicates that a high percentage of adolescent victims must face the location of their assault almost every day.

Contrary to the findings of other studies (Nelson and Amir 1975; Geller 1977), none of the adolescent victims reported that they had been hitchhiking prior to the assault. This finding, derived from a large number of assault experiences over a three-year period, suggests that for the adolescent population at least, hitchhiking is not a major factor in the occurrence of sexual assault.

With very rare exception, the assaults involved only one victim and one offender. Across the three-year period, only twelve victims reported being assaulted by more than one offender and only fifteen reported that they were not the only victim. These cases are clearly atypical, although they are important from the standpoint of understanding the effect of this type of assault experience on victim response and adjustment.

All victims were asked to respond to a list of factors that could have precipitated the assault (see appendix C). The factors ranged from offender and victim characteristics and behavior to the time of day or location. A majority of victims in all three years cited the time of day and the fact that the offender was sexually excited as major causal factors. A large proportion also indicated that the location of the assault and the offender's being drunk or high contributed to the occurrence of the assault. Not surprisingly, over 75 percent of the victims in each of the years attributed no responsibility for the assault to their behavior, dress, or physical appearance. From the victim's perspective, situational factors and the offender's behavior are seen as the primary precipitating factors for the assault.

Offender Characteristics

In 1978, more than 50 percent of the male offenders were in the sixteen to nineteen age range; by 1980 only about one-third were in this age group, and over 50 percent were twenty years of age or older.

In 1978 and 1979, only 8 percent of the victims did not know their offenders. By 1980, this percentage had risen to 17 percent, suggesting that as the adolescents moved into young adulthood, their chances of being assaulted by a stranger increased. In the majority of instances across all three years, the offender was either the boyfriend or the date of the victim. To a lesser extent, the offender was a friend or an acquaintance.

These data on offender characteristics as reported by the victims lend some insight into the interrelationships between the adolescent victim and her offender. First, they indicate that the majority of adolescent sexual assaults occur between individuals in approximately the same age range. It does not appear from these findings that adolescents are being assaulted, to

The Victim's Perspective

any large degree, by adults. Second, the fact that the offender in the majority of the assaults was a date or a boyfriend defines the central context within which adolescent sexual assault occurs. Without a doubt, the dating situation provided the setting in which most female adolescents were sexually assaulted in the late 1970s.

Force and Pressure Experienced

The amount of types of force and pressure experienced in the assault were of major interest in this research. To measure this, each victim was asked to indicate whether any of eleven specific types of force or pressure had been used on her. The types of force ranged from verbal persuasion and threats to physical beating, choking, and injury from a weapon (see appendix C for the actual wording). Table 4–1 summarizes the findings from this item by presenting the proportion of victims from each year who reported each type of force.

The two types of force reported by the largest proportion of victims in all years were verbal persuasion and the size and strength of the offender(s). In addition, from 27 percent to 40 percent of the victims in each year indicated that they had experienced some pushing, slapping, and mild roughness. The other types of force were reported to a much smaller degree, most not exceeding 20 percent in any year.

Table 4–1, shows that several types of force were reported by an increasing proportion of victims across the three years surveyed. The pro-

Table 4–1
Proportion of Victims Reporting Each Type of Force, 1978–1980

Type of Force	1978 (N = 62)	1979 (N = 63)	1980 (N = 47)
A. Verbal persuasion	58 (1)	65 (1)	55 (2)
B. Verbal threats of blackmail	11	8	13
C. Verbal threats of injury	10	13	21
D. Size and strength of offender intimidates	39 (2)	59 (2)	66 (1)
E. Number of offenders intimidates	8	5	4
F. Victim was drugged or gotten drunk	15	19	23
G. Victim was taken by surprise	11	8	36
H. Pushing, slapping, mild roughness	27 (3)	38 (3)	40 (3)
I. Display of a weapon	5		15
J. Physical beating and/or choking	5	8	15
K. Injury from a weapon	2		4

Notes: The rankings within each year for the three most-common types of force experienced are in parentheses.

Each victim could report as many types of force as were experienced. Hence, the percentages do not add to one hundred because each victim may be included more than once.

portion of victims reporting verbal threats of injury more than doubled from 1978 to 1980, and the proportion indicating that they were drugged or gotten drunk was two-thirds again as large in 1980 as in 1978. Some of the more-serious forms of physical force evidence large increases over this same period as well: a three-fold rise in the reports of physical beatings and/or chokings, for example. Although there were no reports of the display of a weapon or injury from a weapon in 1979, the proportion reporting these experiences in 1980 was approximately three times what it had been in 1978.

Table 4–2 synthesizes these data by combining the individual types of force into four general kinds of force: verbal, situational, threat, and physical. These are loosely ranked from the least to the most serious. Victims are represented in this table by the most-serious kind of force they report. Hence a report of both threats and physical force will be recorded under the physical force only as that was the most-serious kind experienced.

The data in Table 4–2 show that the proportion of victims experiencing only verbal force declined by more than 50 percent over the three years. While the proportion reporting situational force as the most serious they experienced remained relatively constant over this period, a slight increase was noticeable in the proportion reporting threats. Most striking, perhaps, was the sizable increase in the proportion reporting some physical force. Forty-three percent reported this type of force in 1980, whereas only 29 percent had in 1978. What appears to be an escalation of the seriousness of the force experienced was confirmed by an analysis comparing victims from each year on the most-serious force reported. Although there were no significant differences between the victims from 1978 and 1979 on this variable, significant differences between the victims from 1980 and those from the two earlier years were observed. A significantly higher proportion of the victims in 1980 reported physical force than in the other two years combined.

The data presented in Tables 4–1 and 4–2 suggest that as female adolescents grow older, the types of force and pressure they are likely to experi-

Table 4–1

Proportion of Victims Who Reported Each Type of Force as the Most Serious They Experienced, 1978–1980

Type of Force[a]	1978 (N = 62)	1979 (N = 63)	1980 (N = 47)
Verbal (items A and/or B)	39	21	17
Situational (items F and/or G)	10	10	11
Threats (items C, D, E, and/or I)	23	29	28
Physical Force (items H, J, and/or K)	29	38	43

[a]See table 4–1 for a listing of the items in each type of force.

ence in a sexual assault change substantially. While verbal persuasion still is reported by a majority of the victims, a much larger proportion report physical force than in the earlier years. These findings are not surprising since the greater mobility of older adolescent females, as well as their association with older males, increases the probability that they will confront some physical pressure for sex.

Victim Resistance and Outcome

In order to assess victim resistance, all victims were asked to describe what they did, if anything, to try to prevent the assault. The answers were grouped into several categories, which had been developed from information gathered in a pretest (see appendix C). These categories ranged from reasoning with the offender to physically resisting to running away. The question posed to the victims did not presuppose that all victims would resist, so it was possible to answer by explaining why no action was taken to prevent the assault.

Most victims employed several techniques in an attempt to resist the assault. The three approaches reported by the largest proportion of victims in each of the three years were reasoning with the offender (from 43 percent to 48 percent), becoming hostile and angry (from 32 percent to 45 percent), and physically resisting (from 28 percent to 39 percent). Across the three years, the 1980 victims (who as a group experienced more physical force) had the highest proportionate response in each of the following categories: becoming angry and hostile (45 percent), screaming and yelling (28 percent), and using excuses to deter the offender (17 percent). The proportion of 1980 victims who physically resisted is about the same as in the other years. While this may seem surprising, the fact that proportionally more of them experienced physical force from the offender may have deterred or prevented them from physical resistance.

Only about 5 percent of the victims in each year indicated that they offered no resistance at all. The primary reasons for not resisting were being scared or afraid or being intimidated because of a relationship with the offender. From 0 percent to 4 percent indicated that their lack of resistance was due to their being intoxicated or high on drugs.

In all three years, a majority of the victims were successful in deterring the assault or other factors prevented the assault from being completed. Not surprisingly, the largest proportion of completed assaults occurred in 1980. Approximately one-third of the assaults described by the 1980 victims were completed, while only about 20 percent were in each of the previous two years.

Summary

In reviewing these descriptive data, it is important to recall that they are reflective only of the most-recent event experienced in each year. To the extent that most victims had only a single assault or that the most-recent event was representative of all the assaults experienced, these data may be generalized to all assaults reported for 1978 through 1980. Caution should be exercised in drawing this conclusion, however.

Most of the assaults described occurred in a vehicle or in the offender's or the victim's home. Data available only in 1980 suggest that a high proportion of victims were assaulted in their own neighborhood. None of the victims reported that they were hitchhiking when the assault occurred.

In most instances, the assaults involved one victim and one offender. Multiple-offender assaults were very rare. The offender was a date or boyfriend in a majority of the cases in each year. In 1980, however, the proportion of cases involving an unknown assailant rose substantially. Because a majority of the victims were eighteen years of age or older in 1980, they were generally out of the home and in work or college settings where the chances of being assaulted by a stranger were higher. Nonetheless, the data clearly indicate that adolescent victims are most often assaulted in a dating situation, by someone they know, who is in their same age range. This pattern begins to change only as the youth become young adults and start to move into new environments.

With regard to the amount and type of force experienced, verbal persuasion and the size and strength of the offender(s) were the two types reported by the largest proportion of victims in all three years. The lowest level of physical force (pushing, slapping, and mild roughness) was reported by from 27 percent to 40 percent of the victims in each year. The proportion of victims mentioning some of the more-serious types of force such as physical beatings and injury from a weapon increased two to three times from 1978 to 1980.

One noticeable trend over this time period was an escalation in the seriousness of the force experienced by the victims. A significantly higher proportion of the victims in 1980 reported physical force than in the other two years combined. In dating situations, older adolescents are more at risk than their younger counterparts of encountering the use of physical force to secure demands for sex.

Most victims used a variety of techniques to thwart the offender. Reasoning with the offender, becoming hostile and angry, and physically resisting were the three approaches reported by the largest proportion of the victims in all years. Very few victims offered no resistance, and this is probably a major factor in the high proportion of assaults that were not completed. Inasmuch as the 1980 victims experienced significantly more force than the victims from the previous two years, it is not surprising that a higher proportion of them were unable to deter the offender.

Overall these data draw a picture of adolescent sexual assault as occurring primarily within the context of a date. It does not appear that the majority of these assaults involve serious, physical force or conclude with physical injury to the victim. In fact, most probably would be classified as attempts since most of the victims indicated that the assault was not completed.

If this profile does not fit the stereotypic one of a teenager being sexually attacked by a stranger while hitchhiking or by an acquaintance met while drinking in a public place, it is probably because that picture is inaccurate for the majority of assaults or attempted assaults that adolescents experience. Most teenage females are far more likely to be confronted with the possibility of a sexual assault from someone they date than from a stranger they encounter in a public place.

Given this situation, what are the personal consequences to an adolescent of facing or experiencing a sexual assault from someone she presumably liked and chose to spend time with? How does she react to this situation, and what are the behavioral and emotional effects of this experience? Are these effects short-lived or of longer duration? What factors in the assault itself, in her environment, or in her relationships with family and peers influence her adjustment process and how? The next chapter explores these issues in some depth in an attempt to outline and describe the initial and long-range consequences an adolescent faces after a sexual-assault experience.

Note

1. This sample of 172 cases is slightly smaller than that used in the prevalence estimates because cases where the respondent refused to answer the sexual-assault questions ($N = 1$) or where the interviewer forgot to ask these questions ($N = 2$) are included in the prevalence estimates but cannot be included here.

5
The Aftermath of Sexual Assault

In the wake of a sexual assault, victims act and react in a multitude of ways. Immediate needs may include responding to personal feelings and injuries (if any), deciding whether to report the assault to the authorities, parents, and/or friends, and in general attempting to manage the situation. With time, the incident may be forgotten, lose its emotional and behavioral impact, or become a serious impediment to everyday functioning, as well as to social and psychological development. How the adolescents in the study responded to their sexual-assault experiences, both initially and over some period of time, is the subject of this chapter.

In interpreting the data in this chapter, it is important to remember that a victim's life history and personality may be as important in explaining reactions to a sexual assault as her current environment and features of the assault itself. Since we do not know the history of these adolescents prior to the inception of the study, it is not possible to know which have been victimized previously or have other unique life experiences that may affect their reactions to an assault. Although we comment on observed relationships between individual responses and features of the assault or other personal factors measured during the course of the study, we do so recognizing that the findings are confined to that time period and the variables we were able to measure and analyze.

Reports to the Police

One of the most-immediate decisions a victim must make is whether to inform the police of the sexual assault. Given the high number of attempted date rapes and the fact that sexual assaults typically are not reported to the police, it is not surprising that only 5 percent of the assaults from 1978 through 1980 were reported. This amounts to an exceedingly small number of cases in any single year and precludes any detailed annual analyses. By combining the reported cases across the three years and comparing them to those sexual-assault cases that were not reported, however, some limited observations and comparisons may be made.[1]

When comparing the types of assaults that were reported with those that were not, some factors emerge that could have influenced the decision made. Over the three years, a substantially higher proportion of the reported cases involved an unknown assailant (41 percent as opposed to 8 percent) and multiple offenders (33 percent versus 6 percent). Threats of violence and actual physical violence occurred in twice the proportion of reported as opposed to nonreported sexual assaults. With one exception, all of the sexual assaults reported to the police contained some physical violence, and in several incidents the victims were threatened and/or injured with weapons. Furthermore, while only 21 percent of the nonreported assaults were completed, approximately 56 percent of the reported assaults were.

A further understanding of the elements involved in the reporting decision may be gained by examining the stated reasons for the decision made. The reporting group indicated that fear of the offender and a desire to prevent him from future assaults were primary reasons for reporting to the police. The nonreporters cite their relationship with the offender and the fact that the assault was not completed as explanations for not telling the authorities. These rationales coupled with the actual differences in the nature of the assaults experienced suggest that attempted assaults by dates or boyfriends may not be defined by the victims as legitimate assaults for purposes of official reporting and only assaults of a more stereotypic nature (those involving a stranger and physical violence) are likely to be reported to the police.

In summary, it is reasonable to suggest that most adolescent victims do not report their sexual-assault experiences to the police because they do not perceive them as legitimate (they do not involve strangers or substantial violence) or because the assault was not completed. Other research on adolescent sexuality (Zellman et al. 1981) has indicated that contemporary teenagers expect and receive a fair amount of pressure for sex in dating situations. This expectation may lead them to accept as normative sexually aggressive, assaultive behavior unless it occurs outside a dating situation or becomes especially violent. If a higher threshold has been established by adolescents for defining forced sexual behavior as sexual assault, the underreporting of this behavior to the police may be substantial.

Effects on Personal Relationships

Much of the research on adolescent sexual assault indicates that personal relationships with parents, friends, and others are often jeopardized by a sexual assault (Burgess and Holmstrom, 1974; McCahill, Meyer, and Fischman 1979). Reactions of significant others to the victim and the assault experience may substantially affect the victim's ability to cope with the situation. Bonds of trust and communication may break down under attempts to comprehend the situation and assign blame. Consequently victims are often ambivalent about telling parents and others of the experience because they fear negative reactions as well as desire support and reassurance.

Not surprisingly, only a small proportion of the victims in our study told their parents about their sexual-assault experience. Over three-quarters of the victims did not inform their parents. Those parents who were told almost uniformly expressed concern and support, as well as anger at the offender and some fear for the victim. Not more than 5 percent directed any anger or blame at the victim or questioned the truthfulness of the account, according to the victim reports.

One additional piece of information about the consequences of informing parents also suggests that support rather than censure may be the more-typical parental response. All victims who told their parents were asked whether their relationship with them had changed as a result of the sexual assault, and if so, how. Over 40 percent of these victims cited positive changes, such as closer than before and more trusting, as indications of an improved rather than damaged relationship; however, a small proportion (from 8 percent to 15 percent) did indicate that their parents were less trusting and thought less of them than before the sexual assault. Also 75 percent of the victims reported that their parents were more protective than previously, and this change could be interpreted as both positive and negative. Overall the response of parents who know about the assault was supportive and directed toward helping the victim rather than blaming or rejecting her. No general conclusions about parental reactions may be drawn from these findings, however, since they are based on such a small and probably unrepresentative sample.

In contrast to the situation with parents, over two-thirds of the victims reported their sexual victimization to their friends. In line with general perceptions about peer support, friends were consistently concerned and supportive. Less than 5 percent of the victims reported any negative reactions from friends, and over 60 percent reported that their friendships became more personal. Inasmuch as so few victims told their parents or sought help from other sources, friends appear to be the primary source of support for adolescent victims. These findings imply that adult participation in the adjustment process for teenage victims may be limited. This could mean that certain kinds of emotional and behavioral reactions may go unnoticed and untreated for some period of time.

In summary, these findings show that where parents and friends know of the assault, they are generally supportive and nonjudgmental. The assault experience does not appear to have any negative effects on the victim's relationship with her parents other than possibly to make them more protective. Relationships with friends appear to be strengthened by the sharing of information about the assault. The data also indicate that less than one-quarter of the parents were told of the assault, whereas three-quarters of the victim's friends were. From these results, one would have to conclude that sexual-assault victims confide primarily in their friends. The price of not telling parents in terms of stress and anxiety was not measured; however, it is hard to imagine that there is not some negative effect.

Aside from relationships with friends and parents, those with husbands and boyfriends also may be seriously affected by a sexual-assault experience. Whether the husband or boyfriend is the offender or only an affected party, the assault, if known, is bound to have an influence on the nature of the relationship. To assess this influence, questions were asked about the victim's dating or marital status at the time of the assault, and when appropriate, the role of her husband or boyfriend in the assault and the effect of the assault on the relationship. These questions were asked only in 1979 and 1980.

When asked if they were married, living with someone, or dating someone special, 63 percent of the victims in 1979 and 1980 said yes. This subgroup of victims became the group of interest for answering questions about the effect of a sexual assault on romantic relationships. Of this group, over half (52 percent) indicated that the offender had been their spouse or boyfriend. Of these victims who were sexually assaulted by someone with whom they were romantically involved, two-thirds stated that the relationship had changed because of the assault. For most of this group, the change was an end to the relationship; 87 percent reported that the relationship terminated as a direct result of the assault.

It is interesting but not surprising that one-third of the victims assaulted by their romantic partners reported no change in their relationships as a consequence of the assault. The research on wife battering and sexual assault by dates and husbands consistently has shown a reluctance on the part of victims to alter or end assaultive relationships. That so many of the victims did terminate the relationships may be attributed to the dating context and the fact that the majority of the relationships were not contractual but mutually consenting ones, thus more easily terminated by either party.

Those victims who were not assaulted by their husband or boyfriend were faced with the decision of whether to inform them of the assault. Approximately 63 percent of the victims did so and met with the following reactions: 91 percent of the husbands and boyfriends were concerned, 87 percent were angry at the offender, 83 percent were supportive, and 65 percent were shocked as well as fearful for the victim. Less than 5 percent disbelieved or rejected the victim, but 17 percent blamed the victim, and over one-quarter were angry at her. As to changes in their relationship as a result of the sexual assault, a majority of the victims reported that they were closer and more affectionate than before. Nonetheless, approximately 25 percent indicated that there was less trust and that their partner thought less of them than before the sexual assault.

Overall these data suggest that personal relationships with husbands and boyfriends may not be seriously affected by a sexual assault unless the perpetrator was the husband or boyfriend. In these cases, the relationship has a high probability of ending. The findings indicate that about 20 percent of the husbands or boyfriends directed anger and blame toward the victim. In general, however, romantic partners not responsible for the sexual assault appear to express support and concern for the victim.

Effects on Personal Behavior

To assess the effect of the sexual assault on their typical behavior and routine, the victims were asked a series of questions about how the sexual assault influenced their involvement in a variety of activities, including working, community and school activities, studying, athletics, and dating and social affairs. The only category in which more than 20 percent indicated they had changed their involvement was dating and social affairs. Approximately 22 percent stated that they had decreased their dating because of the sexual assault. About 15 percent indicated that their involvement in work and studies had slacked off as a consequence of the sexual assault. A specific query about quitting school (or stopping for a while) generated only a 5 percent positive response. In general, the majority of the victims did not report that the sexual assault provoked major changes in any of the activities listed.

Given that the majority of the assaults occurred in dating situations, were not extremely violent, and did not result in completed assaults, it is not surprising that they produced so little change in the school, work, and community involvements of the victims. The effects of adolescent sexual assaults of the kind typified in this research may be primarily emotional and psychological rather than behavioral.

One additional behavioral result of a sexual assault may be to seek counseling. To learn about this experience, we asked the victims if they had consulted any of a large number of individuals, including but not limited to medical doctors, school personnel, rape-crisis-center staff, and psychiatrists. For any of the people they had consulted, we inquired how helpful these individuals had been.

Very few had approached any professional counselors or practitioners. The school-personnel category was cited by twelve victims, two-thirds of whom indicated that they had received quite a bit to a great deal of help from these people. Nine victims consulted crisis-center counselors, six sought medical advice, and four reported seeing a psychiatrist. Almost uniformly, those victims who sought help from professional counselors or practitioners felt they had received it. In terms of helpfulness, the lowest-rated group was the doctors; one-third of those seeking help felt they got none or very little from these professionals.

Not surprisingly, the individuals consulted by the largest number of victims were friends (seventy-four victims mentioned this group) and relatives other than parents (twenty-nine victims sought their counsel). The helpfulness ratings were quite high for these two groups.

These findings are generally what might be expected given the nature of the assaults and the age of the victims. Counsel is generally sought from peers rather than professional people or even relatives. These results strongly suggest that most adolescent sexual-assault victims are not sharing their concerns with any adult figures or seeking any professional counseling. While this may seem appropriate given the typical assault experience, it also may mean that serious emotional problems go unnoticed and untreated for some time.

Initial Reactions

To gain some sense of the victims' immediate reactions to the assault, all victims were asked to describe their feelings within a week of the incident. This was done by asking all victims to respond to a standard set of possible reactions to the assault (see appendix C). Since the assaults had already occurred and the victims were being asked to recall their feelings, these initial reactions are retrospective. Depending on the month of the most-recent assault, this procedure involved a recall of from one to twelve months. The typical recall period was six months or less, however, since over 70 percent of the most-recent assaults had occurred in the last six months of each year. Despite the different recall periods, analyses indicate there are not significant differences in reactions by length of recall. Given this finding, no controls were employed for length of recall.

Table 5–1 shows by year the proportion of victims who experienced each of the individual reactions within a week of the assault. For each of the three years, the primary initial reactions are anger, embarrassment, depression, and guilt. The proportion of victims reporting all of these feelings with the exception of guilt increases each year from 1978 to 1980. The proportion reporting feelings of guilt increases from 1978 to 1979 but is relatively stable thereafter.

For each year, all of the fear reactions such as fear of being alone and fear of other men are reported by a lesser proportion of victims than the reactions just described. As the victims get older and the assaults involve more force and unknown assailants, fearful responses increase. For example, while in 1978 only 16 percent of the victims reported fear of other men

Table 5-1
Proportion of Victims Who Reported Each Reaction within a Week of a Sexual Assault, 1978–1980

Reactions	1978 (N = 62)	1979 (N = 63)	1980 (N = 47)
Fearful of the offender's return	23 (5)	37 (5)	36
Fearful of other men	16	27	47 (5)
Fearful of being alone	23 (5)	30	30
Fearful of having sex again	18	23	38
Feel guilty	40 (4)	52 (4)	51 (4)
Feel embarrassed	48 (2)	56 (3)	66 (2/3)
Feel depressed	42 (3)	57 (2)	66 (2/3)
Feel angry	63 (1)	75 (1)	89 (1)
Feel worth less as a person	13	22	33
Not interested in having sex again	10	18	30

Note: The rankings within each year for the top five reactions are given in parentheses.

within a week of the assault, by 1980 almost half of the victims cited this reaction (47 percent). By 1980, all of the fear reactions were reported by 30 percent or more of the victims, while none of the fear reactions was cited by even a quarter of the victims in 1978.

Given the greater amount of force experienced and the larger number of completed assaults in 1980, perhaps it is not surprising that the largest proportionate response to almost all the reactions occurs in that year. For some feelings, such as not interested in having sex again, feeling worth less as a person, and fearful of other men, the response is double or triple what it was in 1978.

In summarizing these findings, some general observations come to mind. First, despite the fact that the majority of the assaults were not completed and involved dates or boyfriends, a large proportion of victims reported negative emotional and psychological reactions within a week of the incident.

Second, the large proportion reporting some guilt over the incident reflects the ambivalence that many sexual-assault victims seem to have about their role in the assault. Inasmuch as social and cultural conditioning place primary responsibility on the female for controlling sexual outcomes, failure to exercise that control may provoke guilt feelings. Even in 1980 when the generally more-serious character of sexual assaults would seem to militate against the victims' assuming much responsibility for the assault, over half of the victims still expressed feelings of guilt.

Finally, the data in table 5-1 clearly indicate that the proportion of victims reporting negative reactions within a week of the assault increases substantially from 1978 to 1980. The explanation for this linear increase may be found primarily in two factors: age and the seriousness of assaults experienced. As adolescents mature, so generally do their self-concepts and social skills. Consequently it may be easier for older victims to understand and express their negative reactions to a sexual assault than when they were younger and less confident of themselves and others' responses to them. In addition, the more-serious nature of the assaults in 1979 and 1980 logically should generate more-negative reactions.

First Follow-up

In addition to describing their reactions within a week of the assault, victims were asked to indicate how they felt about the assault at the time of the interview. Depending on when the assault occurred, this set of responses reflects personal reactions anywhere from one to twelve months after the assault. In reality, the lag period from the most-recent assault to this first follow-up is more likely to be from one to six months since about three-quarters of the described assaults in all three years occurred from July through December. Analyses of victims divided by length of recall period (one to three, four to six, seven to nine, or ten to twelve months after the assault) showed no significant differences in reactions as a function of time from assault. Hence reactions will be presented by year but with no control for length of recall.

Table 5-2 shows the proportion of victims reporting each type of reaction from one to twelve months after the sexual assault. Without exception, these proportions declined substantially from those indicated within a week of the assault (table 5-1). For some reactions such as depression, anger, and guilt, two to three times fewer victims reported having these feelings at the time of the interview as opposed to within a week of the assault. Overall there is no question but that initial reactions diminished sharply even for those most recently assaulted.

Despite the declining proportions, the relative rankings among the top five reactions remain approximately the same. Even as many as twelve months after the assault, anger is still the reaction reported by the largest proportion of victims, followed by embarrassment. Guilt has replaced depression as the response reported by the third largest proportion of victims, however. Across all years, the proportion of victims reporting any fear reactions dropped sharply. Only in one year (1979) do any of the fear reactions draw more than a 20 percent response, whereas in table 5-1, almost all of the fear reactions reached that level or higher.

The observed pattern in table 5-1 of increasing proportions on most of the reactions from 1978 to 1980 is not noticeable in the figures in table 5-2. Despite displaying the highest proportionate response to most of the reactions within a week of the assault, the 1980 victims look like their 1978 and

Table 5-2
Proportion of Victims Reporting Each Reaction from One to Twelve Months after a Sexual Assault, 1978-1980

Reactions	1978 (N = 62)	1979 (N = 63)	1980 (N = 47)
Fearful of the offender's return	11	10	11
Fearful of other men	11	11 (5)	13
Fearful of being alone	13 (5)	24 (2/3)	17 (4/5)
Fearful of having sex again	11	11 (5)	4
Feel guilty	19 (3)	13 (4)	23 (3)
Feel embarrassed	31 (2)	24 (2/3)	26 (2)
Feel depressed	18 (4)	21	17 (4/5)
Feel angry	42 (1)	51 (1)	64 (1)
Feel worth less as a person	8	10	6
Not interested in having sex again	5	10	11

Note: The rankings within each year for the top five reactions are given in parentheses.

1979 peers at the first follow-up with the exception of their high anger response. These findings do not suggest that the initially different reactions among the groups stand up over time or may necessarily have been related to the more-serious nature of the assaults experienced by the 1980 victims. With the possible exceptions of anger and embarrassment, it would appear that the typical assault experienced by most adolescents (an attempted assault by a date) does not generate reactions that persist even for a period of a year.

This is not to say that certain subgroups of adolescent victims might not have serious reactions and adjustment problems or that longer follow-up periods might not evidence some different patterns from those portrayed here.

Differential Response to a Sexual Assault

In order to assess the effect of personal characteristics and the nature of the assault on victim reactions, we needed to maximize the number of cases with particular features. No single year had sufficient distributions on all of the variables of interest to permit an adequate test. Hence, we decided to combine cases across the three years, if possible, to maximize sample sizes and distributions on the relevant factors. A priori, there was no reason to believe that the victims and/or their sexual-assault experiences should be substantially different by the year of report, particularly since the three years were consecutive. The basic questions presented to the victims were standard across all the years so the stimuli were consistent. We felt that if the yearly victim groups were not significantly different on demographic characteristics, features of the assault, or initial reactions, it would be possible to combine them without obscuring important period differences. If successful, this procedure would permit the maximum sample size possible for the analyses relating victim reactions to personal characteristics and the nature of the assault.

The effort was only partially successful because the 1980 victims did turn out to be significantly different from the 1978 and 1979 ones on several dimensions. Although not differing on demographic variables, the 1980 victims were substantially different in terms of the nature of the assault and reactions to it. In particular, they experienced significantly more force than did the 1978 and 1979 victims, and a significantly higher proportion of them were assaulted by strangers. There were also significant differences between the two groups on both immediate and more long-term reactions. On the basis of these results, we decided to combine the victims from 1978 and 1979 but not those from 1980.

In the process of combining these two victim groups, two other issues arose. First, although theoretically it would have been possible to combine all of the sexual-assault cases from these two years, the fact that a number of victims reported in both years or also had reported an assault in the first two years of the NYS (in 1976 or 1977) introduced a confounding factor. We have scant knowledge about reactions to a single sexual assault, let alone any appreciation of the possible interactive influence of multiple assaults over a period of years. Therefore to simplify interpretation of the findings, two basic procedures were followed. First, all victims who reported an assault in 1976 or 1977 or both years as well as in 1978 or 1979 were excluded from this sample. Second, victims who reported an assault in both 1978 and 1979 were included in the analyses only for their first known report (the one in 1978). Because we do not know about any sexual assaults prior to 1976, these procedures do not ensure that only victims of a single assault will be included. To the best of our ability, however, they do exclude those cases with multiple assaults over several years for which interpretation of reactions may be the most difficult.

A second complicating factor was that although some victims reported only in one year, they reported more than one assault in that time period. In an effort not to diminish further the size of the sample by automatically excluding these cases, several analyses were run comparing the single- and multiple-assault groups. The groups were compared on several sociodemographic variables, as well as their reactions to the assault within a year of its occurrence. No significant differences were observed. Furthermore, the multiple assaults appear to be primarily the result of continual pressure from dates and/or boyfriends for sex rather than repeated violent sexual assaults within a year period. Given these findings, we decided to maintain in the sample the victims who reported more than one assault in the year of their first assault. We acknowledge that this may introduce some noise into the interpretation of findings but felt the advantages of a larger sample outweighed this concern, especially since no significant differences were discovered on several key variables.

Once all of these conditions had been met, a sample of ninety-five first-time victims from 1978 and 1979 was created. This sample was used to explore the effects of personal characteristics and the nature of the assault on reactions to the assault. To begin, the group was divided on the basis of the elapsed time from the assault to the interview (one to three months, four to six months, seven to nine months, or ten to twelve months after the assault). This was done to determine whether victim reactions would differ as a function of the length of the recall period. No significant differences were observed either on immediate reactions (within a week of the assault) or those reported at the time of the interview. This finding suggested that it would not be necessary to control for length of recall, and hence no control was employed.

Reactions within a week of the assault and from one to twelve months later were analyzed by a series of personal as well as assault variables. Individual reactions such as guilt, depression, and anger were analyzed, as well as summary measures reflecting a cumulation of all the reactions.

Immediate and more long-term reactions were not differentiated by race, age at the time of the assault, place of residence (urban, suburban, or rural), or social class. These results from the chi-square tests and t-tests imply that initial reactions and those within a year of the assault are not significantly influenced by the sociodemographic characteristics of the victims.

To assess the impact of different assault experiences, a series of factors associated with the kind of assault were examined. The assault variables analyzed included number of offenders, relationship between victim and offender, whether the assault was completed, summary measure of force experienced, most-serious force experienced, and type of resistance offered. Victim reactions were significantly differentiated on only a few of these variables.

First, those victims who were able to prevent the assault clearly experienced fewer reactions within a year of the assault than did victims who could not stop the assault. Although no substantial differences were observed on the reactions reported within a week of the assault, those reported at the first follow-up (from one to twelve months later) were significantly different by whether the victims had deterred the assault. A significantly higher proportion of the victims of completed assaults as opposed to those of deterred assaults reported guilt and depression at the first follow-up: 29 percent versus 9 percent and 35 percent versus 12 percent, respectively.

Initially the total amount of force experienced during an assault appeared to have a substantial impact on reactions both immediately and within a year. Victims were divided into three groups depending upon the amount of force they reported: low, medium, or high.[2] Significantly more of the victims in the last group reported embarrassment and depression within a week of the assault than did victims who reported moderate force. However, there were not significant differences between the extreme categories because the low-force group reported higher mean reaction scores than the moderate-force group.

This same situation was true for the reactions reported at the first follow-up. The highest proportion of yes responses to feelings of guilt, anger, depression, and embarrassment one to twelve months after the assault came from the high-force group. The lowest came from the moderate-force group, with the low-force group reporting intermediate scores. Again, the significant differences, this time on guilt, embarrassment, and depression, were between the high and moderate groups. These findings suggest that while there is an empirical relationship between the amount of force experienced in an assault and reactions to that assault, the relationship is not simple or linear and could be spurious. Possibly some other variable or variables accounts for the significant differences between the moderate- and high-force groups. Demonstration of this remains elusive, however, because the small sample sizes preclude controlling for more than one variable at a time.

Overall the only variable that produced consistent, significant differences in reactions was whether the assault was completed. Victims who were able to deter the assault reported substantially fewer negative reactions within a year of the assault than did those who were assaulted. None of the demographic variables examined affected the reactions reported. We suspect that the relative homogeneity of the assault experiences may have precluded the possibility of discovering any real differences in reactions. It is also possible that the variables examined are not the most relevant.

To conclude the analyses with this constructed sample, we decided to assess the changes in reactions from the initial report to the first follow-up. Since so few of the personal or assault variables significantly affected the reactions of the victims, we chose to look at trends in reactions over time for the entire victim group by comparing the mean initial reaction scores with those reported at the first follow-up.

Almost without exception, all of the individual reactions declined significantly from the first to the second report. The declines were significant at the .05 level of probability or less. None of the mean scores increased from the first to the second report, and only two, fear of being alone and not interested in having sex again, remained relatively stable. These results suggest that many initial reactions to the type of assault experiences reported in this study diminish substantially within the period of a year. The two reactions that did not decline, fear of being alone and not interested in having sex again, represent potential problems for the behavioral and sexual development of adolescent victims.

Long-Term Reactions to a Sexual Assault

Of the ninety-five victims in the previous sample, thirty-six became victims in 1978 for the first time in the study and reported no additional assaults in 1979 or 1980. This is the group that has the potential for the longest follow-up period (without any intervening assaults) since their reactions could be obtained in 1979 (some thirteen to twenty-four months after their assault) and again in 1980 at twenty-five to thirty-six months after their assault. Of these cases, thirty-four responded to the follow-up questions in 1979 and thirty-one to the same questions in the 1980 survey. Thus 86 percent of this sample (31 cases) have follow-up data for up to three years after their sexual-assault experience. This is the sample we used to examine long-term reactions to sexual assault.

For initial reactions and each of three follow-up periods, table 5-3 shows the proportion of the long-term sample who reported each of the reactions. Within a week of the assault, the reactions reported by the largest proportion of victims were anger, embarrassment, depression, and guilt, in that order. Twenty-three percent of the sample reported fear of the offender's return, fear of other men, and fear of being alone. At the first follow-up, one to six months after the assault for two-thirds of the victims, the proportion reporting each of the reactions had declined, substantially so in the case of several of the reactions. The four reactions reported by the

Table 5-3
Proportion of 1978 Victims Reporting Each Reaction at Four Time Periods after a Sexual Assault

Reactions	Initial Reactions within a Week (N = 31)	First Follow-up, 1-12 Months Post[a] (N = 31)	Second Follow-up, 13-24 Months Post[a] (N = 31)	Third Follow-up, 25-36 Months Post[a] (N = 31)
Fearful of the offender's return	23	10	10	0
Fearful of other men	23	13	10	16
Fearful of being alone	23	16	39 (3)	36 (3)
Fearful of having sex again	19	13	10	7
Feel guilty	42 (4)	23 (3)	19 (4)	10
Feel embarrassed	58 (2)	35 (2)	45 (1)	52 (1/2)
Feel depressed	45 (3)	19 (4)	10	19 (4)
Feel angry	61 (1)	39 (1)	42 (2)	52 (1/2)
Feel worth less as a person	13	6	3	7
Not interested in having sex again	10	6	3	7

Notes: This table includes only the 1978 victims who reported no additional assaults in 1979 and/or 1980.

The rankings within each follow-up period for the top four reactions are in parentheses.

[a]Since two-thirds of the long-term sample reported that their assaults occurred in the last six months of 1978, the follow-up periods for most of the sample are at least six months less than the maximum shown for each period.

largest proportion of victims, however, remained virtually the same as within a week of the assault. These results are comparable to those for the full sample of 1978 victims presented in Tables 5-1 and 5-2.

By the second follow-up period, some interesting changes begin to emerge. Most noticeable is the fact that 39 percent of the victims report fear of being alone, whereas only 23 percent had reported it within a week of the assault and even less (16 percent) at the first follow-up. A second unusual pattern is that the proportion reporting embarrassment and anger has increased from the first follow-up, although it is still less than in the beginning. All other reactions show a declining or stable relevance in the lives of victims.

By the final follow-up, some two to three years after the assault, only one of the reactions originally reported (fear of the offender's return) has been extinguished completely. The proportion reporting several other reactions has increased from the second follow-up period, almost doubling in the case of depression, and more than doubling for the reactions of feeling worth less as a person and not interested in having sex again. Embarrassment also shows an increase from the second to third follow-up period, though it is not nearly as great. Of more significance may be the fact that the proportion of victims reporting fear of being alone is greater at the final follow-up than at the initial one. Some two to three years after the assault, the proportion of victims reporting this fear is almost double that indicated within a week of the assault. This finding clearly implies that some responses to an assault that appear mild initially may intensify with time. Thus, relatively short follow-up periods may not pick up some substantial effects because they have a long incubation period or are suppressed initially. These findings certainly suggest that follow-up data on sexual-assault victims are needed for as long as two-to-three years after an assault in order to document the full range and pattern of reactions.

In order to assess whether the observed changes in reactions were in fact significant, a series of analyses were conducted comparing the individual reactions at each time period with those at each subsequent follow-up. Significant differences were observed on several comparisons. From within a week of the assault to the last follow-up period, four of the reactions evidence significant declines at the .05 level of probability or less: fear of the offender's return, fear of having sex again, feel guilty, and feel depressed. No other significant differences were observed except on the reaction, fear of being alone. From the first to the final follow-up, there was a significant increase in the proportion of victims reporting this reaction ($p \leq .01$).

To summarize, over the four assessment periods, there appear to be two distinct trends among the reactions assessed. First, as might have been predicted, several of the reactions were reported by the largest proportion of victims right after the assault, and the proportions declined fairly steadily thereafter. At two to three years after the assault, all of the reactions evidencing this pattern were reported by significantly fewer victims than initially. Fear of the offender's return, fear of having sex again, and feeling guilty all fit this profile.

This second trend is more curvilinear in that the proportion reporting is high initially, declines in the middle, and rises again at the last follow-up. Several of the reactions, including anger, embarrassment, depression, and fear of being alone, fit this pattern, although the curves for each of these reactions are not identical. This type of curvilinear pattern suggests a resurgence of feelings and reactions some two to three years after the assault, which is hard to explain without more-specific data. There is some acknowledgment of this pattern in the work by McCahill, Meyer, and Fischman (1979). They speculate that adolescents are less likely than adults to experience adjustment problems in the year following their assault for two primary reasons. First, they can more easily alter the behavioral patterns that may have led to the assault than can adults, who are often locked into routines associated with work and family. Second, the transitional stage of life they are in allows them to anticipate moving away from the setting and interaction patterns surrounding the assault experience. The authors argue, however, that assault-related problems are not avoided entirely by youth; they are simply postponed until the youth mature and are faced with the development of more-serious heterosexual relationships. Although this reasoning may account for some of the curvilinear patterns observed, it does not explain these patterns for younger victims who are in mid-adolescence at the two- to three-year follow-up. Furthermore it does not explain why only some reactions follow this trend.

A logical course of action at this point would be to analyze the reaction patterns by several features of the assault or personal characteristics of the victims. While the small sample size and uneven distributions on key variables preclude a reliable statistical analysis of this type, some general observations may be offered from a case-history perspective. All the cases with initial reactions and three follow-ups were reviewed ($N = 31$).

The most-compelling conclusion from this exercise was that reaction patterns to an assault are not systematically ordered by the nature of the assault experience or by any of the social or demographic variables analyzed. Victims with very comparable assault experiences in terms of number of offenders, relationship to the offender, force experienced, and outcome reported very different reactions both initially and over time. Sociodemographic variables such as race, social class, and place of residence did not appear to affect reactions consistently. The effect on reactions of differential responses by parents and friends could not be assessed adequately since there was almost no variance on these factors; most victims had not told their parents and had told their friends. These findings imply that other factors such as history of traumatic events and differential support by significant others may play a more-important role in influencing reactions to an assault than the character of the assault itself or the demographic profile of the victim.

One unexpected finding from the review of individual cases was that so many victims of attempted assaults by dates or boyfriends reported fear of being alone and fear of other men, often two to three years after the unsuccessful assault. Preconceptions had led us to believe that these fear reactions would persist only for victims of serious, physically rough assaults (assaults involving strangers, weapons, and/or physical violence). While it is the case that victims of these kinds of assaults do report fear reactions as well, it was surprising how often they were reported by victims of attempted date rapes that involved little physical force. This type of sexual assault is fairly common among the adolescent population and appears to be an almost standard feature of dating. If a sizable proportion of female adolescents react to these attempted seductions with some generalized fears, the effect of these seemingly mild sexual experiences may be more serious than previously imagined.

One final observation from the case-history review is that the reaction data from the second and third follow-ups may partially reflect a testing effect. Comments from several victims suggested that they had almost forgotten the assault, and one concludes they might have without prompting. If this conjecture is correct, the reactions reported by these victims may be artifacts of the repeated interview situation and not meaningful fears or feelings that actually affect their lives. While it is impossible to know whether a testing effect is present or how strong it is, there is at least a suggestion in the data that it might be. This problem is intrinsic to longitudinal panel designs, and we have tried to take it into account when interpreting the long-term reaction data.

Notes

1. These comparisons will be limited in two specific ways. First, so few cases were reported to the police from 1978 through 1980 ($N = 9$) that we were not able to control for prior assaults, prior experience with the police, and other factors of relevance to the reporting decision. Second, these comparisons may be made only on features of the assaults and not on personal characteristics of the victims. As a consequence of cumulating three years of data to increase the sample size, the reporting and nonreporting victim groups are not independent. This is because victims of multiple assaults across three years may report to the police in one instance and not

The Aftermath of Sexual Assault

in another. Hence, analyses of group differences on individual variables such as race and social class are not appropriate.

2. The total force score was derived in the following manner. Each type of force was scored one or zero depending on whether it was reported. Then each type of force was weighted according to how serious it was, using the following scheme:

Type of Force	Weight
Verbal persuasion	1
Verbal threats to reveal	1
Drugged or gotten drunk	2
Taken by surprise	2
Verbal threats of injury	3
Person was bigger and stronger	3
More than one person	3
Display of weapon	3
Pushing, slapping, and mild roughness	4
Physical beating and/or choking	4
Injury from a weapon	4

The potential range of scores is from 0 to 30; the actual range is approximately 0 to 21. The actual distribution of scores was split into thirds, producing low-, medium-, and high-force groups. Scores associated with these groups are as follows: low = 1, medium = 2–5, and high = 6 or more.

6 Vulnerability to Sexual Assault

Of all the issues related to sexual assault, perhaps none generates more-intense interest than that of vulnerability. It touches every woman, and there are few who have not thought about their own vulnerability to this crime. Beyond the individual level, however only in the last two to three decades have sociologists and social psychologists begun to develop theories to account for the distribution of rape and sexual assault observed in different groups and populations. These explanations range from global, social-structural arguments to more-limited ecological or subcultural perspectives.

At the broadest level, it has been argued that all women are vulnerable because of the sharp sexual stratification in most societies and the female socialization process, which trains women to be submissive and acquiescent. Rape and sexual assault are viewed as the natural outgrowth of power relationships that emerge when sexual stratification is marked within a society (or within major subgroups within a society). It is acknowledged that cultures or societies (as well as subgroups within) may vary in the degree to which they are sexually stratified, and hence vulnerability to sexual assault should vary as well. Although these arguments from feminist and conflict theory have not received much empirical testing, recent research by Sanday (1981) and Williams and Holmes (1981) has begun to fill this gap.

Less-global theories of vulnerability to sexual assault have focused on ecological and subcultural themes. These approaches argue for differential risk on the basis of such factors as low socioeconomic status, minority-group membership, residence in a high-crime area, and the existence of subcultures of violence (Amir 1971; Curtis 1976). To a large extent, these explanations are based on victim data generated from criminal-justice, hospital emergency-room, and rape-crisis-center files. The disproportionate number of lower-class, minority women found in these samples, for example, has led to theorizing that these groups face a higher risk of sexual assault.

All of these theories have some currency and support, but they generally have not been verified on representative samples of women. Knowledge about vulnerability to sexual assault is still tied to known or officially reported cases, which are unlikely to be typical of all sexual-assault cases. Comparisons of victims and nonvictims derived from a general population survey are needed to determine whether the images we have of victims, created partly from feminist ideology and partly from official records, are in fact accurate.

To address this issue, one objective of the SAP was to use the national probability sample of adolescents to test some generally stated ideas about vulnerability to sexual assault. The availability of a representative sample of adolescents, which contained a reasonable sample of sexual-assault victims, offered a unique opportunity. By comparing the victims to a control group on several factors believed to be related to vulnerability to sexual assault (race, social class, sex-role attitudes, a deviant life-style), some understanding of the concept of differential risk could be achieved.

This effort was viewed as exploratory, and consequently no single theoretical framework was imposed. Two theoretical perspectives pervade this effort, however, one by happenstance and one by choice. The NYS, the larger study out of which the SAP grew, has as a primary objective a test of an integrated theory of delinquent behavior. This theory incorporates a number of sociopsychological concepts, including strain, commitment, and conventional and delinquent bonding. Although these variables are not generally part of the theorizing about risk of sexual assault, it seemed reasonable to take advantage of their presence. Consequently we included in the victim-control comparisons several of these factors.

By choice, we decided to analyze the risk of sexual assault from a sex-role perspective. Within the sexual-assault literature, two of the basic themes regarding risk of sexual assault are tied to this perspective and yet are inherently contradictory. On the one hand, it is argued that females who conform to the traditional female role model are more vulnerable to sexual aggression because of their passivity and general acquiescence to male demands (Brownmiller 1975; Gager and Schurr 1976; Weis and Borges 1973). On the other hand, it is asserted that liberated women face a higher risk of sexual aggression because of their nonconformity and violation of traditional norms for female behavior (Adler 1975; Hayman 1972; Lee 1972). This circular reasoning leads to two, alternative conclusions: (1) all women are equally at risk of a sexual assault, regardless of their sex-role attitudes and behavior, or (2) traditional and nontraditional sex-role attitudes are related. While both of these positions seem untenable (certainly neither is supported by the available data), it is less than clear what role, if any, sex-role attitudes and behavior play in affecting vulnerability to sexual assault.

In an effort to address the inconsistencies in the literature and to assess empirically the impact of sex-role attitudes and behavior on sexual assault, we chose to conceptualize vulnerability in sex-role terms and to test this scheme with the sexual-assault data.

Conceptualization of Vulnerability

Sexual-assault literature, especially that influenced by feminist analyses (Brownmiller 1975; Gager and Schurr 1976; Griffin 1971), has stated that the role of the traditional female, resulting from conventional female socialization, is structurally conducive to assuming the role of rape victim. From childhood, females learn to be submissive and subordinate, to direct their attention toward being attractive and appealing rather than assertive and competitive (Weitzman 1975). This identification process is operative in all major social institutions (home, school, and the peer group), as well as being supported by image reinforcement in the mass media. The result of this comprehensive socialization process, according to some researchers, is that women become vulnerable to sexual aggression because of their propensity, ingrained by conventional sex-role training, to acquiesce to such behavior. Weis and Borges (1973) define the socialization process of the female as one that molds her into a victim and provides the procedure for legitimizing her in the role. Similarly Russell (1975) argues that acceptance of the feminine mystique increases a woman's risk of rape.

Other researchers provide empirical evidence that women are often ambivalent and passive in the face of sexual aggression. In a study on male sexual aggression on a university campus (Kirkpatrick and Kanin 1957), it was noted that an ambivalent resistance was often offered by college women who encountered sexual aggression. While a large number expressed anger, their responses were more often characterized by indecision, guilt, and embarrassment. In another study assessing potential responses to a sexual assault, female respondents were much less likely than male respondents to select a physically aggressive response to a hypothetical assault (Tolor 1977).

Despite the pervasiveness of this argument, we are not convinced that traditional sex-role socialization is related to vulnerability to sexual assault. In the first place, if the female socialization process is as universal as the perspective implies, there would be no variability on this factor, and thus it could not help to explain differential vulnerability to sexual assault. However, the assumption that all or most females in our society experience the same type of sexual socialization is unjustified. The socialization process is not necessarily traditional, complete, or identical for all women. Race and class status, among other factors, influence and differentiate sex-role socialization, as has been described most recently by Williams and Holmes (1981). Thus it is possible, in line with the sex-role perspective, that those most traditionally socialized are more at risk of a sexual assault; however, we think it as likely that vulnerability to sexual aggression and assault is tied to unconventional sex-role attitudes as to traditional ones. Women whose attitudes flaunt or denigrate traditional sex-role patterns and norms may be equally at risk. In sum, we are inclined to believe that sex-role attitudes are not strongly related to risk of a sexual assault. This is not to say that sex-role attitudes may not contribute to a sexual assault or interact with other factors to increase vulnerability, but we do not expect that their contribution will be primary.

The second major theme focuses on the impact of sex-role behavior and, in particular, inappropriate role behavior, on vulnerability to sexual assault. Women whose behavior is inconsistent with that typically expected of them by society have often been considered open to sexual aggression. It is argued that women who go out alone at night, frequent bars, and display other atypical female role behavior are more likely to be sexually assaulted than those who behave in accordance with traditional expectations (Lee 1972; Hayman 1972). Women who overplay their sexuality (according to some undefined set of social norms) or use it for economic gain are believed legitimate victims (they are said to have precipitated their own victimization). The belief that certain women have created their own vulnerability by their unconventional and deviant behavior is widespread and has been reinforced by the findings from several studies.

Results from a survey of Michigan policemen indicate that most of these men charged with enforcing the sexual-assault laws believe that some women deserve to be raped (Pope 1974). Additionally, a study assessing judicial attitudes toward rape victims (Bohmer 1974) indicates that judges feel there are types of women who are raped because they are asking for it. Furthermore, there are innumerable studies involving rape cases indicating that such factors as the victim's previous sexual experiences, marital status (divorced women are less likely to be believed than married ones), and relationship with the offender often influence juries to acquit (Cann, Calhoun, and Shelby 1977; L'Armand and Pepitone 1977; Kalven and Zeisel 1966; Jones and Aronson 1973). Finally, there are suggestions throughout the literature that adolescent women who engage in such deviant activities as running away from home, hitchhiking, drug use, and frequent sexual intercourse are, by the nature of these activities and the environments they occur in, setting themselves up for a sexual assault (Nelson and Amir 1975; Konopka 1976; Russell 1975; Robert 1966).

Besides involvement in delinquent or deviant activities, assuming a liberated sexual life-style may also increase a female's vulnerability to sexual assault. The more-open sexual attitudes associated with changes in conventional female roles may make men expect sexual intercourse and be less likely to accept refusals (Adler 1975). Williams and Holmes (1981) argue that the occurrence of date rapes may increase as a result of liberated behavior on the part of women:

The liberated woman is often sexually active and will not rely on moral or virginal protestations to reject a sexual advance. As a result, situations in which unsuccessful seductions become rapes—"date rapes"—are likely to increase. If a woman says "no," it is likely a matter of personal choice and as Weis and Borges note, "since both participants 'lose face' when the refusal is blunt and without the usual justifications, the rejected suitor may take it as a personal attack" (1973:97) and respond with physical force.[1]

While there appears to be rather widespread support both in the literature and among the public for this argument, no sound data indicate that women who behave in unconventional ways are in fact more vulnerable to sexual victimization. Data on the frequency of antisocial behavior among groups of known rape or sexual-assault victims are incomplete or nonexistent. More important, no controlled data are available to ascertain whether victim rates of such behavior are comparable to those of nonvictims from the same race and class groups. Without such data, the evidence that atypical female role behavior raises the risk of sexual assault is inferential at best. We assumed that there would be no significant relationship between these two factors.

To summarize, data from SAP will be used to explore the relationship between sex-role attitudes and behavior, and risk of sexual assault. We anticipate that these factors will not significantly influence vulnerability to sexual assault. The data also permit an assessment of the influence of race and social class on the risk of sexual assault. Several other general attitudinal and behavioral variables tied to an integrated delinquency theory will be assessed as well. Comparisons will be made on these variables between victim and nonvictim groups.

Analysis Procedures

To reduce the disparity in sample size between the female victim group and all nonvictimized females in each year, we developed some procedures to select a control group from the sample of females who had not reported any sexual assaults in each year. In each year, all females who reported no sexual assaults as either a victim or offender were eligible for the control group. The victim and control samples were matched only on sex because to match on any other variables could have obscured potential differences between victims and nonvictims. For each year, systematic samples of approximately the same size as the female victim group were drawn from the nonvictim, nonoffender female sample. For each year (1978, 1979, and 1980), statistical comparisons were conducted between these control groups and the samples from which they were drawn on a number of relevant variables: age, social class, race, and self-reported delinquency. No significant differences were observed. Although these tests cannot ensure that no biases are present in the control groups, they do indicate that the control groups are representative of the larger samples from which they were drawn, at least on the variables examined.

In order to determine whether female, adolescent sexual-assault victims may be distinguished from the nonvictimized female youth population, a series of t-tests (and chi-square tests where appropriate) was conducted. These analyses were undertaken with several variables. The two key variables, Attitudes toward Sex Roles and Deviant Life-style, were measured in the following ways. First, the sex-role scale was designed to assess the extent to which adolescents adhere to traditional expectations regarding appropriate role behavior for men and women. The intent of the scale was to focus on both behavior and characteristics of men and women, as well as role responsibilities of each gender within their relationships with each other. (A description of this scale as well as its psychometric properties is found in appendixes A and B.) The second variable was measured by general reports of involvement in all types of delinquent behavior, as well as by a specially constructed Deviant Life-style measure. This measure was composed of five deviant behaviors often cited in the literature as related to adolescent sexual assault: running away from home, hitchhiking, prostitution, sexual intercourse, and being drunk in a public place.

In addition to the two specific variables, all of the basic sociodemographic variables were examined (race, age, social class, and place of residence). Comparisons were made as well on a large number of environmental, atittudinal, and behavioral measures (described in appendix A).

Victim and Control-Group Comparisons, 1978–1980

1978 Comparisons

None of the sociodemographic comparisons produced any statistically significant differences. Also most of the attitudinal and behavioral measures did not evidence substantial differences between the victim and control groups. In particular, the two groups were not differentiated on the Sex-Role Attitudes scale. Some significant differences were observed, however, on measures related to the peer group. The victims had a significantly more-delinquent peer group than the controls ($t = -3.99$, $p \leq .00$). Regarding involvement in delinquent behavior, the victims received significantly less disapproval from their peers than the controls received from their peers ($t = 2.57$, $p \leq .01$). Although there was no significant difference between the victims and the controls on the scale Attitudes toward Deviance, the peer-group findings suggest that the victims are more exposed to delinquency from their peers, both attitudinally and behaviorally.

While no significant difference appeared on the General Delinquency scales or on the Deviant Life-style measure, the victim and control group are differentiated on several of the offense-specific scales. Of the delinquency scales analyzed, the four presented in table 6–1 show significant differences. In all cases, the sexual-assault victims were substantially more delinquent than the control group. It is obvious from the size of the standard deviations, however, that there is considerable overlap in the distributions. While the mean values of the two groups are statistically distinct on these scales, it is unlikely that there is much predictive power in these differences.

A final measure on which we compared the groups was the total amount of nonsexual victimization experienced. The data in table 6–1 clearly indicate that the controls experience substantially less victimization of all kinds than do the victims.

In summary, the data indicate that female adolescent sexual-assault victims in 1978 are not distinct from nonvictims demographically or on either the Sex-Role Attitudes scale or the Deviant Life-style scale; however, the victims engage in delinquency and are supported in this behavior by their peers to a significantly greater extent than the control-group members. They also have experienced significantly more nonsexual victimization than the controls.

On the basis of these data alone, one would conclude that attitudinally and demographically, female sexual-assault victims are not particularly distinguishable from their nonvictimized peers. Their involvement in delinquent behavior and the character of their peer groups, however, do differentiate them from the controls. It may be that these features affect vulnerability to sexual assault or are simply idiosyncratic to the 1978 victims. The data from 1979 and 1980 may offer an answer.

Table 6–1
Significant Mean ($\bar{X}$) Differences between Victims and Controls on Self-Report Delinquency and Victimization Scales, 1978

Scale Name	Victim $\bar{X}$	SD	Control $\bar{X}$	SD	t-Value	p
Minor Assault	1.48	3.78	0.23	0.64	2.59	.01
Minor Theft	0.70	1.92	0.10	0.43	2.42	.05
Crimes against Persons	1.78	4.14	0.32	0.92	2.72	.01
School-related Delinquency	9.90	13.77	4.48	8.77	2.63	.01
Nonsexual Victimization	5.24	9.93	0.89	1.29	3.45	.00

1979 Comparisons

The victim and control-group comparisons on sociodemographic variables evidenced no significant differences by age, race, social class, or place of residence. None of these tests even approached statistical significance. The victim group did experience more disruptive events in their family, such as divorce or extended unemployment than did the control group ($t = -3.16$, $p \le .01$); nonetheless, these data, like those from 1978, suggest that there are not strong, consistent sociodemographic differences between female adolescent sexual-assault victims and nonvictims.

Unlike the 1978 findings, the attitudinal measures showed several significant differences between the two groups, which are summarized along with the self-report delinquency data in table 6-2. The control group was substantially more involved in school academics than were the victims and less likely to believe they had to break rules to achieve conventional goals at school (School Normlessness). The controls also evidence substantially less Normlessness in the family context than do the victims. Furthermore, there

Table 6-2
Significant Mean ($\bar{X}$) Differences between Victims and Controls on Attitudinal and Behavioral Scales, 1979

Scale Name	Victim $\bar{X}$	SD	Control $\bar{X}$	SD	t-Value	p
Family variables						
Family Normlessness	9.38	3.15	8.13	2.64	−2.42	.05
School variables						
Involvement in School Academics	6.88	3.45	8.13	2.98	2.05	.05
School Normlessness	10.59	3.17	9.50	2.43	−2.03	.05
Peer variables						
Importance of Peer Aspirations	15.46	3.54	13.46	3.45	−3.30	.00
Exposure to Delinquent Peers	28.42	7.67	21.69	5.85	5.52	.00
Commitment to Delinquent Peers	4.43	1.28	3.98	1.06	−2.13	.05
Perceived Peer Disapproval of Delinquent Behavior	41.98	6.13	44.93	5.55	2.82	.01
Peer Pressure for Drinking and Drug Use[a]	11.08	3.70	8.51	2.49	−4.58	.00
General variables						
Attitudes toward Deviance	36.78	6.37	40.32	5.15	3.43	.00
Trouble from Drinking[a]	7.12	3.23	5.47	1.26	−3.63	.00
Trouble from Drug Use[a]	6.77	2.89	5.44	1.40	−2.59	.01
Delinquent behavior and victimization						
Felony Assault	0.70	2.34	0.02	0.13	−2.31	.05
Crimes against Persons	4.10	13.15	0.15	0.81	−2.38	.05
Index Offenses	0.86	2.76	0.02	0.13	−2.42	.05
General Delinquency	95.51	140.24	36.32	79.97	−2.90	.01
School-related Delinquency	30.35	55.43	6.83	17.44	−3.21	.01
Nonsexual Victimization	3.79	6.54	0.76	1.28	−3.58	.00

[a]These measures were available for all subjects only in 1979 and 1980.

was a significant difference between the groups on their attitudes toward deviance, with the victims less likely to judge deviant acts as wrong than the controls.

The peer-group findings are similar to, if not stronger than, those from the 1978 data. The sexual-assault victims seemed to view their peer relations as significantly more important than the controls do. Furthermore their peers were substantially more delinquent than those of the controls, and the victims asserted a greater commitment to these peers, even though they were delinquent. The peers of the victims also seemed to provide an atmosphere supportive of delinquency to a substantially greater extent than the peers of the control-group members. Finally, on a new scale available in 1979 and 1980, which measured peer pressure for drinking and drug use, the controls reported substantially less pressure of this type than did the victims.

When self-reported delinquency scores were compared, the victims had higher mean scores than the controls on all of the scales examined. Several of these differences achieved statistical significance (see table 6–2). Unlike 1978, the victims and controls are distinguished here on a general measure of delinquency as well as on a measure of all serious offenses, the Index Offense scale. The mean differences on these two scales between the two groups are substantial and suggest real differences in the levels of involvement in these offenses by the victims and the controls. Again, however, the magnitude of the standard deviations indicates that although the two groups are statistically different on these measures, there is considerable overlap in the scores.

The amount of nonsexual victimization reported by the 1979 victims is significantly higher than that reported by the controls, as may be seen in table 6–2. The victim mean is approximately five times that of the control mean.

In summary, although there are few demographic distinctions between the 1979 victims and controls, there appear to be numerous attitudinal and behavioral ones. The most consistent are: the victims' tendencies to be involved with and supportive of delinquent peers, substantially greater involvement in delinquent behavior on the part of the victims, and a significant difference in the amount of nonsexual victimization experienced by the two groups, with the victims reporting more. Because these three differences were also evidenced in the 1978 comparisons, some patterns are beginning to emerge that may alter our conceptualization regarding vulnerability to sexual assault. It is beginning to appear that deviant behavior, albeit not the specific types included in the Deviant Life-style scale, is related to sexual assault. Sex-role attitudes again did not distinguish the groups, reinforcing our belief that this set of attitudes is peripheral to the risk of a sexual assault. If the 1980 comparisons produce similar results, we will be in a position to define more precisely some factors associated with vulnerability to sexual assault for adolescent females.

1980 Comparisons

As in the previous two years, no significant differences between the victim and control groups were observed on any of the sociodemographic variables; however, the family life of the victims was disrupted by significantly more traumatic events, such as divorce and death, than that of the controls ($t = -2.04$, $p \leq .05$). Thus although the two groups are not demographically distinct, it does appear that the home environment of the victims is substantially less stable than that of the controls.

Significant findings from the comparisons between the victims and controls on several attitudinal, behavioral, and self-report delinquency measures are presented in table 6–3. One pattern in these results indicates that the victims generally had less involvement with their families and poorer

Table 6–3
Significant Mean ($\bar{X}$) Differences between Victims and Controls on Attitudinal and Behavioral Scales, 1980

Scale Name	Victim $\bar{X}$	SD	Control $\bar{X}$	SD	t-Value	p
Family variables						
Family Aspirations-Current Success	16.85	5.12	19.11	4.15	2.37	.05
Involvement in Family Activities	7.26	4.25	9.63	3.42	2.62	.01
Social Isolation from Family	11.19	4.29	9.31	3.14	−2.44	.05
Perceived Negative Labeling by Family	25.67	7.13	22.69	4.94	−2.38	.05
School variables						
Social Isolation from School	11.12	2.77	9.95	2.31	−2.05	.05
Peer variables						
Perceived Peer Disapproval of Delinquent Behavior	40.90	6.86	44.71	5.17	3.07	.01
Exposure to Delinquent Peers	28.72	9.21	20.36	5.89	−5.28	.00
Peer Pressure for Drinking and Drug Use[a]	11.71	4.16	8.15	2.23	−5.22	.00
General variables						
Attitudes toward Deviance	36.65	5.98	39.83	5.22	2.78	.01
Attitudes toward Sex Roles	19.73	5.09	22.13	4.81	2.37	.05
Attendance at Religious Services	2.31	1.32	2.96	1.38	2.34	.05
Trouble from Drinking[a]	7.32	3.18	5.28	0.57	−4.32	.00
Trouble from Drug Use[a]	7.11	3.22	5.13	0.35	−3.68	.00
Delinquent behavior and victimization						
Minor Assault	1.71	4.83	0.08	0.40	−2.32	.05
Public Disorder	30.50	81.14	1.13	2.29	−2.51	.05
Status Offenses	54.19	70.32	13.85	32.12	−3.61	.00
Crimes against Persons	2.29	5.76	0.10	0.52	−2.62	.01
General Delinquency A	103.46	138.67	18.50	36.93	−4.10	.00
General Delinquency B	49.00	73.41	10.63	25.56	−3.42	.00
School-related Delinquency	21.21	36.20	4.08	14.89	−3.03	.00
Deviant Life-style	48.83	88.46	10.65	25.77	−2.87	.01
Nonsexual Victimization	3.90	5.77	0.77	2.00	−3.55	.00

[a]These measures were available for all subjects only in 1979 and 1980.

family relationships than did the control group. Specifically they felt less successful at maintaining a good relationship with their families, were less involved in family activities, and felt more estranged from their families than did the control group.

The data in table 6-3 also confirm the association between victims and delinquent peers that was observed in the 1978 and 1979 findings. The 1980 victims had peers who were less likely to disapprove of delinquent acts, more involved in delinquent behavior, and more likely to approve of drinking and drug use than the peers of the control-group members.

Two final comments about the results reported in table 6-3 seem appropriate. First, the significant difference between the two groups on the Attitudes toward Deviance scale suggests that the victims judge more deviant behaviors as acceptable than do the controls. This finding in conjunction with the peer-group results indicates that the victims are behaviorally and attitudinally more tolerant of delinquent behavior than are the controls. Second, for the first time we see a significant difference between the victims and controls on the Attitudes toward Sex Roles scale. The direction of the scores indicates that the controls hold significantly more-traditional values than do the victims. This finding would suggest that the risk of sexual assault is higher among females who hold nontraditional sex role values; however, no differences between the victims and controls were observed on this scale in either of the other years.

The differences in frequency of self-reported delinquency between the victim and control groups were similar to those reported previously. The victims reported higher mean scores than the controls on all of the delinquency scales, and these differences were significant for the scales listed in table 6-3. This table also reflects the significant differences between the two groups on the scales Trouble from Drinking and Drug Use and Nonsexual Victimization. For these measures, the victims again report the higher scores, indicating more problems from drinking and drug use and more victimization in general.

The 1980 comparisons produce results generally similar to those reported for 1978 and 1979. One slight change is that the 1980 findings indicate that the victims feel isolated from their families, and that the family environment is not stable. This finding was noted in the 1979 results as well, but the estrangement and separation from the family was not reported so strongly then.

General Summary

In summarizing the findings from 1978 through 1980, we have operated with the rule of thumb that significant differences that appear in two or more of the years are likely to reflect real, substantive distinctions between sexual-assault victims and controls. Hence we confine our comments generally to variables that meet this criterion.

Despite some popular beliefs that sexual-assault victims are disproportionately lower-class, minority, urban women, the SAP data show no significant differences between victims and nonvictims on these characteristics. The only demographic variable that differentiated the victims and controls for two or more years was the Family Crisis scale. In two of the three years, the victims reported significantly more disruptive events in their homes such as divorce and extended unemployment than did the controls. Although we have no data from which to argue for a direct connection between this factor and the risk of sexual assault, it may be that this experience interacts with other factors to influence vulnerability. An unstable home environment may leave an adolescent female without the basic emotional and physical support she needs during a period of rapid sexual, biological, and psychological development. If she turns to male friends or dates for this support, her needs may be taken advantage of or misinterpreted. This line of reasoning is conjecture, but the findings do imply that a family environment punctuated by disruptive events may contribute to the risk of sexual assault.

Some of the strongest findings from these analyses are associated with the peer group and involvement in delinquent behavior. For all three years, sexual-assault victims had a significantly higher exposure to delinquent peers and received support from these friends for unconventional, delinquent acts. In addition, the victims themselves were significantly more involved in a wide variety of delinquent behavior, including serious offenses. They also reported significantly more trouble from drinking and drug use than did the controls. Not surprisingly, in two of the three years the victims reported receiving significantly more peer pressure for drinking and drug use than did the controls. In line with their behavior, the victims display far more-tolerant attitudes toward deviance than do the controls.

Although the findings are somewhat inconsistent, it does not appear that sex-role attitudes play a major role in differentiating victims from controls. In two of the three years examined, no significant differences were noted between the two groups on this scale. Where a difference did emerge, it was consistent with the behavioral findings in that the victims were more nontraditional in both attitudes and behavior. We conclude from these results that sex-role attitudes are unrelated to the risk of a sexual assault but that deviant or inappropriate role behavior is.

Taken in concert, all of these findings indicate that engaging in delinquent behavior and being part of a delinquent network influence the risk of being sexually assaulted (and victimized in other ways as well). Although the specific delinquencies previously associated with sexual assault (hitchhiking, prostitution, running away from home, and so forth) do not significantly differentiate victims from controls, the two groups are distinctly different in terms of the character of their peer networks and their involvement in general and serious delinquency. It appears that teenage females who are generally delinquent are advertising their unconventionality in ways that jeopardize their control of sexual situations. If one is behaviorally and attitudinally delinquent, conventional protestations with regard to requests for sexual intercourse may fall on deaf ears. Confining a delinquent image to nonsexual behavior may not be possible.

Previctimization Comparisons

If victims and controls can be distinguished after the assault has occurred, one obvious question is whether those differences existed prior to the assault and might in some way account for the different experience of the two groups.[2] Most sexual-assault research projects cannot address this question adequately because they have no prospective data (those gathered prior to or simultaneous with the report of an assault). In this case, we are fortunate that the SAP grew out of a larger study that had collected two years of data on all subjects before the research on sexual assault was formally begun. Consequently we are able to compare victims and controls two years before victimization on a number of variables, particularly some of those on which they differed significantly in the year of the assault.[3]

The comparison groups consist of all victims in 1978 who had not reported a sexual assault in 1976 or 1977 and a group of controls who reported no sexual assaults across the entire study period.[4] The data in table 6-4 reflect significant mean differences between these two groups for the years 1976 and 1977 on several attitudinal variables.

The data show that several of the variables that separated the groups after the sexual assaults did so as much as one to two years prior. The victims appear to be less well bonded than the controls, both at home and at school, though the differences between the two groups are not consistently significant. Regarding their peer networks, the victims consistently reported greater exposure to delinquent peers and approval from these peers for illegal behavior. In addition, the victims reported substantially more-tolerant attitudes toward deviance in both 1976 and 1977. While these peer and attitudinal differences did not translate into any significant differences in delinquent behavior in 1976 and 1977, the victims do consistently report higher mean frequency scores on all of the delinquency scales in these years.

The peer differences between the groups persist into 1978, when the first sexual assaults were reported. Furthermore in that year we observed several significant differences between all of the 1978 victims and the controls on some of the delinquency scales (see table 6-1). In all instances, the

Table 6-4
Mean Differences between Future Sexual-Assault Victims (V) and Controls (C) on Selected Attitudinal Scales

			1976					1977			
Scale Name	V	SD	C	SD	t-Value	p	V	SD	C	SD	t-Value	p
Family and school variables												
Family Normlessness	9.19	2.82	8.06	2.42	−2.16	.05	8.46	2.95	7.75	2.23	−1.39	NS
School Normlessness	11.05	2.97	10.50	2.80	−0.96	NS	10.77	2.81	9.70	2.61	−1.98	.05
Peer variables												
Perceived Peer Disapproval of Delinquent Behavior	35.04	6.33	37.98	5.39	2.52	.01	36.12	5.10	38.09	4.91	1.98	.05
Exposure to Delinquent Peers	17.01	6.26	14.71	5.14	−1.92	NS	17.40	5.54	14.11	3.95	−3.31	.00
General variables												
Attitudes toward Deviance	31.18	4.20	33.10	3.13	2.64	.01	30.98	4.08	32.44	3.31	1.99	.05

Note: The victim group is composed of all victims who reported a sexual assault for the first time in the study in 1978 ($N = 55$). To ensure that the controls had no reported sexual assaults across the entire study period, the control group from wave 5 was used ($N = 48$).

victims reported significantly higher levels of involvement in delinquent behavior than did the controls.

These findings suggest that the cumulative effect of associating with delinquent peers and engaging in a fair amount of delinquency may be to raise the risk of sexual assault substantially. We speculate that there are two primary reasons why this may be so. First, the settings and circumstances in which delinquency occurs are likely to be conducive to many forms of deviance. For example, even though a female victim may have intended only to steal some drugs and get high with her friends, the situation could easily evolve into one that ends with a forced sexual experience. Second, a female involved in delinquent behavior may project a generally deviant image, which carries with it expectations about sexual behavior. Consequently she may not be successful in restricting her deviant behavior to nonsexual acts.

Overall the data in table 6-4 indicate that victims and controls are substantially different in terms of peer networks and attitudes toward deviance at least two years prior to the first reported assaults. The victims also appear to be less well integrated into home and school environments than are the controls. Although there are not any significant differences in delinquency between the victims and controls prior to any reported assaults (in 1976 and 1977), the victims always report higher involvement. By 1978 when the first assaults are reported, the two groups are statistically separated on several delinquency scores, as well as many of the peer variables.

While these results imply that certain factors such as exposure to delinquent peers may be predictive of sexual assault, we have not conducted any formal analyses to test this idea. Thus, we completed a discriminant analysis to see how well the variables we have been discussing would do in discriminating the victims from the controls. Seven variables were used in the analysis: Exposure to Delinquent Peers, Attitudes toward Deviance, Perceived Peer Disapproval of Delinquent Behavior, Family Normlessness, and the self-reported delinquency scales Crimes against Persons, Public Disorder, and School-related Delinquency (see appendix A for a complete description of each of these measures).

The discriminant analysis was conducted on the 1978 victims with no prior assaults ($N = 55$) and a control group with no reported assaults throughout the entire study period ($N = 48$). Data for 1977 were used in the analysis so that we could assess the ability of the variables to separate the two groups prior to the occurrence of any sexual assaults.

Only four of the variables evidenced any statistical ability to distinguish between the two groups: Exposure to Delinquent Peers, Attitudes toward Deviance, Crimes against Persons, and Public Disorder. Among these, Exposure to Delinquent Peers was by far the most powerful; its contribution to the discriminant function was four times that of any of the other variables. These four variables, however, were not very successful in assigning the individual cases to the correct groups; only 57 percent of the victims and 67 percent of the controls were correctly classified using these variables. Furthermore, as the total variance existing in the variables is less than 10 percent (eigenvalue = 0.075), these factors cannot be considered very useful for discriminating between victims and controls.

In conclusion, while victims and controls may be distinguished prior to an assault by such factors as peer networks and deviance attitudes, these variables do not accurately predict who will be victimized and who will not. Being delinquent and operating in a delinquent environment is clearly related to sexual victimization, but it is not sufficient, in and of itself, to predict this outcome accurately. It seems likely that the ability to account for the occurrence of sexual assault rests on the integration of a number of variables, only some of which have been measured and analyzed here. A much more detailed and comprehensive research effort is needed before we can identify the constellation of factors leading to sexual assault.

Are Sexual-Assault Victims Unique among Assault Victims?

Among violent personal crimes, it has generally been assumed that sexual assault is in a special category because of its sexual component. Similarly, victims of sexual assault often have been viewed and treated differently from female victims of other physical assaults. Yet to our knowledge, no empirical data support this premise. In fact researchers in the rape and sexual-assault area have commented on the need to compare sexual-assault and other assault victims in order to understand better the risk of experiencing either kind of assault (Katz and Mazur 1979). Knowledge of differences or similarities between these victim groups may indicate whether vulnerability to sexual assault is any different from that to assault in general.

To address this issue, we compared the sexual-assault victims with victims of other physical assaults. We used the first report of an assault, either sexual or not, from the years 1978 through 1980. The nonsexual-assault group was identified by a response of one or more to any of the following questions: "How many times in the last year (1) has something been taken directly from you, (2) have you been beaten or threatened with a beating and/or (3) have you been attacked with a weapon?" To avoid the potentially confounding influence of prior assaults on later attitudes and behavior, we excluded from this analysis anyone who reported an assault, sexual or otherwise, in the first two years of the NYS (in 1976 or 1977). We compared three groups: sexual-assault victims only ($N = 39$), nonsexual-assault victims only ($N = 80$), and victims of both types of assault within the same year ($N = 13$). These three groups were compared on a number of demographic and attitudinal variables, as well as on their self-reported delinquency. In all analyses, the data come from the year of the reported assault(s).

Demographically the three groups are not distinguishable. We found no significant differences by race, social class, age at the time of the assault, place of residence, or number of family crises. Comparisons on three attitudinal scales, Attitudes toward Deviance, Attitudes toward Sex Roles, and Attitudes toward Interpersonal Violence, produced no significant differences among the groups. The only differences were noted on the behavioral measures. On two of the self-reported delinquency scales, Damaged Property and Home-related Delinquency, the victims who had experienced both types of assault reported significantly higher involvement than either of the other assault groups ($p \leq .05$). No significant differences were observed between the groups on the other behavioral variable examined, Exposure to Delinquent Peers.

While variables other than those examined may differentiate the victim groups, there is nothing in these findings to suggest that they are distinct from one another. In fact, the only significant findings placed the two single assault groups together and differentiated them from the victims of both kinds of assault, as might have been expected. Overall these results imply that sexual-assault victims are not substantially different from other physical-assault victims demographically or on a variety of attitudinal and behavioral measures. There is nothing in the factors analyzed to specify the risk of sexual assault from that of other kinds of physical assault.

Notes

1. Joyce E. Williams and Karen A. Holmes, *The Second Assault: Rape and Public Attitudes* (Westport, Conn.: Greenwood Press, 1981), p. 10. Reprinted with permission.

2. Some of the variables that differentiate the groups after the sexual assaults were measured concurrently with the report of a sexual assault. Thus, for example, differences on the self-report delinquency scales reflect differences between the victims and controls that occur simultaneously with the report of a sexual assault. However, most of the distinguishing variables reflect differences between the two groups after the sexual assault had occurred.

3. We were unable to compare the two groups on the Attitudes toward Sex Roles scale since it was not added to the interview until 1978.

4. When the SAP began in 1978, we expanded the set of questions that could identify victims. In 1976 and 1977, there was only one question about being sexually assaulted. Therefore it is possible that some of the victims who reported in 1978 would have reported earlier if the broader set of questions was in use.

**Part III
The Adolescent Offender**

7
The Nature and Extent of Sexual Assault Committed by Adolescent Males, 1978-1980

Prevalence and Incidence Estimates

The procedures for calculating estimates of the incidence and prevalence of sexual assault committed by adolescent males are the same as those employed for the female-victim estimates. Thus we did not include in the estimates any of the reports from potential offenders who deselected themselves at the beginning of the sexual-assault questions. Furthermore we used the nonredundant frequency count for the incidence estimates to preclude the possibility of double counting the same incident. These procedures should help ensure that the estimates are based on only legitimate, independent reports of sexual assaults.

The data in tables 7-1 and 7-2 are based on self-reports of sexual assaults.[1] Since this behavior is both illegal and socially unacceptable, it is to be expected that some underreporting has occurred. The validation analyses for all delinquent acts presented in chapter 2, indicated that both underreporting and overreporting occurred. The former appeared to be the more-serious problem. Consequently the upper ends of the .95 confidence intervals probably contain the more-accurate estimates.

The proportion of male youth who report committing one or more sexual assaults for the years 1978 through 1980 is displayed in table 7-1. For the same time period, table 7-2 depicts the average number of sexual assaults committed by each male adolescent. Age, social-class, race, and place-of-residence estimates are presented in both tables. The data apply specifically to adolescent males aged thirteen to nineteen in 1978, fourteen to twenty in 1979, and fifteen to twenty one in 1980.

The findings suggest that the prevalence and incidence of sexual assault declined over the period examined. Both the proportion of adolescent males committing sexual assault and the frequency of these incidents dropped as the sample of males matured from thirteen to nineteen years of age in 1978 to fifteen to twenty-one years of age in 1980. While it could be argued that this decline is a simple function of maturation, an examination of the same age groups within different birth cohorts shows the decline as well. For example, the proportion of seventeen year olds who reported commit-

Table 7-1
Proportion of Male Youth Who Report Committing One or More Sexual Assaults by Age, Social Class, Race, and Place of Residence, 1978–1980

		1978			1979			1980	
	N	Proportion	.95 Confidence Interval	N	Proportion	.95 Confidence Interval	N	Proportion	.95 Confidence Interval
Total male sample	863	.038	.023–.053	805	.029	.019–.038	783	.022	.013–.031
Ages by year									
1978 1979 1980									
13 14 15	124	.008*	.000–.024	119	.034	.002–.066	119	.034	.003–.064
14 15 16	123	.016	.000–.040	115	.009	.000–.026	112	.009	.000–.026
15 16 17	127	.031	.000–.063	123	.049	.008–.089	122	.016	.000–.040
16 17 18	136	.044	.003–.086	123	.033	.000–.072	117	.017	.000–.041
17 18 19	127	.079	.025–.132	115	.026	.000–.055	109	.028	.000–.059
18 19 20	125	.032	.001–.063	114	.035	.000–.071	115	.035	.000–.070
19 20 21	101	.059*	.021–.098	96	.010	.000–.031	89	.011	.000–.033
Social class									
Middle	190	.026	.003–.049	176	.028	.003–.054	175	.023	.001–.045
Working	254	.036	.010–.061	233	.026	.005–.047	228	.004*	.000–.013
Lower	370	.035	.016–.054	348	.026	.010–.042	334	.024*	.010–.038
Race									
White	681	.032	.015–.049	627	.021	.011–.031	606	.018	.008–.028
Black	136	.074	.033–.114	133	.053	.027–.078	132	.038	.009–.067
Place of residence									
Urban	213	.028	.009–.047	211	.028	.011–.046	204	.025	.004–.045
Suburban	372	.043	.020–.066	343	.029	.012–.046	332	.018	.004–.032
Rural	277	.040	.018–.061	250	.028	.011–.045	242	.025	.006–.043

Notes: Several of the subgroup sample sizes do not add to the total sample N due to missing data or, in the case of race, the absence of the other minority group cases from this table.
Across the three years, the average design effect for the total sample and all subgroups is 1.00.
*Differences significant at $p \leq .05$ for groups so marked.

Table 7-2
Average Number of Sexual Assaults Committed per Male by Age, Social Class, Race, and Place of Residence, 1978–1980

		1978			1979			1980	
	N	Mean	.95 Confidence Interval	N	Mean	.95 Confidence Interval	N	Mean	.95 Confidence Interval
Total male sample	863	0.103	0.047–0.159	805	0.053	0.031–0.076	783	0.037	0.021–0.053
Ages by year									
1978 1979 1980									
13 14 15	124	0.008	0.000–0.024	119	0.067	0.000–0.136	119	0.042	0.001–0.083
14 15 16	123	0.016	0.000–0.040	115	0.009	0.000–0.026	112	0.009	0.000–0.026
15 16 17	127	0.126	0.000–0.289	123	0.081	0.006–0.157	122	0.025	0.000–0.062
16 17 18	136	0.100	0.000–0.208	123	0.065	0.000–0.141	117	0.034	0.000–0.082
17 18 19	127	0.118	0.028–0.208	115	0.035	0.000–0.077	109	0.083	0.000–0.180
18 19 20	125	0.048	0.000–0.100	114	0.061	0.000–0.126	115	0.043	0.000–0.090
19 20 21	101	0.356	0.000–0.719	96	0.052	0.000–0.155	89	0.022	0.000–0.067
Social class									
Middle	190	0.032	0.002–0.061	176	0.045	0.003–0.088	175	0.034	0.000–0.070
Working	253	0.170	0.010–0.330	233	0.060	0.002–0.118	228	0.018	0.000–0.053
Lower	370	0.073	0.011–0.135	348	0.046	0.015–0.077	334	0.036	0.012–0.060
Race									
White	681	0.087	0.024–0.149	627	0.043	0.019–0.067	606	0.036	0.017–0.056
Black	136	0.206	0.044–0.367	133	0.083	0.027–0.138	132	0.045	0.007–0.083
Place of residence									
Urban	213	0.033*	0.011–0.055	211	0.047	0.020–0.075	204	0.039	0.005–0.074
Suburban	372	0.137*	0.046–0.228	343	0.061	0.021–0.102	332	0.024	0.004–0.045
Rural	277	0.112	0.014–0.210	250	0.048	0.012–0.084	242	0.054	0.014–0.094

Notes: Several of the subgroup sample sizes do not add to the total sample N due to missing data or, in the case of race, the absence of the other minority group cases from this table.
Across the three years, the average design effect for the total sample and all subgroups is 1.00.
*Differences significant at $p \leq .05$ for groups so marked.

ting one or more sexual assaults was 8 percent in 1978, 3 percent in 1979, and 2 percent in 1980. Similar though not always linear declines may be noted across the birth cohorts for most other age groups for both the prevalence and incidence data.

Within each year, neither the prevalence nor incidence data show any consistent significant differences by race, social class, or place of residence. In fact the proportionate involvement in each year is almost identical across classes and places of residence. The prevalence differences by race, however, evidence a black-to-white ratio of two to one or greater in each of the three years. Nonetheless the confidence intervals show considerable overlap indicating that the black-to-white distributions are not really separate.[2] Overall we conclude that there is not a significant race differential in the proportion of youth committing sexual assaults. While the proportion of black youth reporting a sexual assault is higher than might be expected, the sampling variance is sufficiently large on what is a relatively infrequent event to preclude statistical significance.

If we had enough cases of violent sexual assaults to analyze separately, we might find a significant race differential. The fact that adolescent victims of such assaults are typically black, coupled with the fact that most sexual assaults are intraracial, leads to the conjecture that a substantially higher proportion of youthful offenders in violent sexual-assault cases may be black. Data beyond those analyzed here are needed to confirm this speculation, however.

Overall these results lead to the conclusion that the proportion of male adolescents committing sexual assaults and the frequency with which these assaults occur has declined from 1978 to 1980. Fewer than half as many males reported committing a sexual assault in 1980 as in 1978; the incidence rate halved over this same period as well. This decline is not a simple function of maturation because the prevalence and incidence estimates for the same-aged groups from different birth cohorts also declined across the three-year period. In addition, the demographic data indicate that the commission of sexual assault is fairly evenly distributed by race, social class, and place of residence.

It is difficult to know how to interpret these results since there are no other national self-report, sexual-assault offender data with which to compare them. The most obvious comparisons might be with the NCS and the UCR, the only other national data sets with offender information (the NCS from victim reports and the UCR from police arrests). Both data sets, however, provide figures for only forcible rape (and attempts), a much narrower set of forced sexual behavior than is included in our study. The inability of the SAP to collect explicit information on the sexual behavior that occurred prevents us from separating out the forcible-rape cases for direct comparison with the UCR and NCS. Nonetheless, in order to place the SAP findings in perspective, some understanding of how they correspond to other national data on rape and sexual-assault offenders seems necessary. While we acknowledge that precise comparisons cannot be made, each data set overlaps the others somewhat, and all three together provide the most-comprehensive current picture of the occurrence of rape and sexual assault.

Comparisons with Uniform Crime Reports and the National Crime Survey

With regard to the incidence of sexual assault and rape committed by adolescent males, the three data sets offer conflicting results. The NCS data for 1978 and 1979 (1980 were not available) show a slight increase in the percentage of forcible rapes perceived to have been committed by youth ages twelve through twenty. According to victim reports, adolescent males accounted for 15 percent of the forcible rapes in 1978 and 21 percent in 1979. The rate of committing forcible rape per 100,000 adolescent males jumped from 120 in 1978 to over 200 in 1979.

Since the UCR do not collect data on the age of the offender as perceived by the victim, it is not possible to know what proportion of the reported forcible rapes were committed by adolescents; however, the UCR arrest data are tabulated by age and permit an examination of the proportion of arrests for forcible rape that are accounted for by adolescent males. It should be noted, however, that only a portion of the rapes reported to the police are judged credible and only a subset of these ever result in an arrest. Furthermore, NCS data suggest that only about half of the forcible rapes described in their surveys are reported to the police. Hence arrest data are at best crude indicators of the incidence of forcible rape during any time period.

From 1978 to 1980, the UCR arrest data show an almost constant rate of arrest for forcible rape for males aged twelve to nineteen: approximately fifty arrests per 100,000 population of adolescent males. There is no indication in these arrest data that the incidence of forcible rape among adolescent males is increasing, as the NCS data suggest. However, we need to remember that these arrest data are several stages removed from the occurrence of the act. All the slippage in numbers due to failure to report initially, a police judgment of unfounded, and failure to make an arrest may drastically distort these incidence estimates.

As would be expected given the differences between the data sets, the self-report sexual-assault data indicate a much higher incidence of forced sexual behavior for adolescent males than do either the NCS or the UCR. In 1978, the ratio of self-reported sexual assaults to arrests for rape per 100,000 males aged thirteen to nineteen was as low as 100 to 1 and as high as 320 to 1 (this range is based on the .95 confidence interval calculated for the self-report data). This gap closes considerably by 1980 but is still 29 to 1 at the low end and 71 to 1 at the high end of the .95 confidence interval. These ratios suggest that the UCR data, which count arrests for forcible rapes, reflect only a small portion of the total amount of forced sexual behavior committed by adolescent males. Acknowledging that the self-report data are conservative estimates only inflates these ratios.

Although the ratios are not as extreme, comparisons between the self-report sexual-assault data and those from the NCS produce ratios ranging from 42 to 1 to 133 to 1 in 1978. Using the .95 confidence interval, these figures indicate that there are from 42 to 133 offender reports of a sexual assault for every one victim report of a forcible rape thought to have been committed by an adolescent male. These ratios become larger in 1979 when the NCS data show a 75 percent increase in the rate of forcible rape by youthful offenders. Here as previously, the large discrepancy between the figures is most likely related to the much broader sexual-assault definition employed in our self-report study. Even comparing the NCS and UCR data sets with a comparable definition of forcible rape, however, the ratio between reported incidence and arrests is nearly three to one in 1978 and over four to one in 1979.

These comparisons indicate that the conclusions we draw about the incidence of rape and sexual assault committed by youth vary considerably depending on the data source consulted. Of the three examined, the UCR is the most limited for estimations of incidence. The number of adolescent arrests for forcible rape is more likely to reflect victim-reporting and police-processing practices than it is the actual occurrence of rape. The NCS offer a far better estimate of the incidence of forcible rape committed by adolescents even though we believe it is low due to underreporting; however, these data reflect only one type of sexual assault and therefore do not capture a large amount of the forced sexual behavior occurring among teenagers.

To the best of our knowledge, the SAP data are the only source for national estimates of the incidence and prevalence of all forced sexual behavior perpetrated by adolescents. Inasmuch as sexual assault is a broader category of behavior than forcible rape, one would expect the SAP estimates to be larger than those derived from the NCS, as they are. The accuracy of these estimates, however, is dependent on the reliability and validity of the self-report data, the representativeness of the sample, and the amount of sampling error. We feel confident about the quality of the sample, but voluntary reporting of illegal and socially repugnant behavior such as sexual assault always carries with it the possibility of purposive concealment. We believe the incidence estimates to be conservative and suggest that the high ends of the .95 confidence intervals may come closer to the actual frequency figures.

In summary, the three data sets each focus on a different part of the rape and sexual-assault picture for adolescents. Individuals interested in the occurrence of forcible rape or arrests for this offense would do well to use the NCS and UCR data sets, respectively. Questions about the broader behavioral category of sexual assault are more appropriately addressed by the SAP data. Our understanding of the incidence of rape and sexual assault among adolescents will be greatly improved by careful and selective use of these data sets depending on our interest.

Comparison of Offender Profiles

The public image of all offenders, including rapists and sexual-assault offenders, is derived primarily from arrest data published annually in the UCR. Whether these data are representative of all offenders is an issue of continuing controversy, which is being addressed by comparing official arrest data with those derived from self-reports of criminal involvement. In this tradition, a comparison of the offender profile generated from the UCR with that from the SAP will be presented.[3] This comparison provides an evaluation of how youth arrested for forcible rape compare with all youth who commit sexual assaults (only a portion of which may be forcible rapes).[4] Although this comparison is limited by the fact that sexual assault encompasses a broader category of forced sexual behavior than forcible rape, it is nonetheless useful as a means of judging how particular data sources influence and shape our image of offenders. Furthermore, since the public perception of adolescent rapists and sexual-assault offenders is based primarily on UCR data, some awareness of how this profile corresponds with one drawn from behavioral data is important.

The annual UCR present information on the sex, age, race, and place of arrest of offenders. For our purposes, we will examine the arrests for forcible rape for individuals eighteen years of age or younger for the years 1978 through 1980.[5] In each of these years, male adolescents accounted for 25 percent or more of all arrests for forcible rape, despite the fact that male youth aged ten to eighteen constitute less than 17 percent of the total male population in the United States (U.S. Bureau of the Census 1980). The racial distribution consistently evidences a disproportionate percentage of black youth; they represent over half of the arrests for forcible rape for youth under eighteen years of age in each of the three years. The UCR also indicate that a higher proportion of urban than rural youth are arrested for forcible rape. In addition, the racial distribution is heightened in the urban arrest statistics because almost 60 percent of the urban youth arrested for forcible rape are black.

From these statistics, it is not hard to see how the image of the typical rapist as a young, black, urban male emerged. Often a lower-class component is added to this profile since other research using selected police arrest data has indicated that rapists are typically from the lower socioeconomic group (Amir 1971; MacDonald 1971; Eisenhower 1969).

Inasmuch as the SAP data reflect behavior rather than arrests and a broader category of forced sexual behavior than just forcible rape, perhaps it is not surprising that the offender profile is so different from that from the UCR. The self-report data evidence no significant differences in the incidence or prevalence of sexual assault by race, social class, or place of residence. Even though according to population distributions, black males are overrepresented in the offender group and whites are underrepresented, these differences are not statistically significant. In contrast to the official profile, the SAP offender profile is not marked by major race, social-class, or place-of-residence distinctions.

In attempting to understand the disparities in the profiles as well as determine the validity and usefulness of each profile, several points need to be considered. First, the UCR profile of youthful rapists typifies only those who have been arrested, and these are only a subset of all youth who commit forcible rape. Of the total number of rapes that actually occur, only those that are reported (NCS and SAP data indicate that 50 percent or more are not reported), are judged legitimate by the police (LaFree 1981 cites evidence to show that this process is affected by judgments about the victim's moral character and conduct), and actually are charged as a rape will appear in police records as legitimate cases of forcible rape. Of this group, only about half will result in arrests. These selective reporting, charging, and arresting processes almost ensure that the final group of arrestees will not be representative of the entire group of offenders. Hence it is safest to treat the UCR profile of adolescent rapists as an arrest profile and nothing more. For this purpose, its validity and usefulness are well established.

The SAP data are distinct from the UCR in several respects. First, the unit of analysis is behavior (number of self-reported sexual assaults), not arrests. Second, all sexual-assault behavior involving forced contact with the sexual parts of the body is included, not just forcible rape. And finally, the data derive from a national probability sample of adolescents. For all these reasons, we would expect the SAP offender profile to differ sharply from the one drawn from the UCR. The SAP profile should be a more-comprehensive and typical picture of the distribution of teenage male involvement in forced sex, assuming we consider the sample to be representative and the data fairly reliable and valid.

Overall what is critical is that distinctions be made between profiles based on arrests as opposed to those generated from behavioral reports. The race and class bias in the forcible-rape arrest statistics reflects the selection process that occurs from the initial reporting to the final arrest. We know from our own and prior research that only the credible assaults (those involving strangers and/or physical violence) are likely to be reported to the police. Victims of these types of assault are more likely to be minority, lower-class women. Assuming that most sexual assaults and rapes are intraracial, the race and even class distribution in the arrest figures is not surprising.

Nonetheless these cases do not reflect all adolescent males who engage in forcible rape, much less all who commit a sexual assault. Self-report data from the SAP and other studies (Kanin 1967a; Smithyman 1978; Polk et al. 1981) do not confirm the official image of adolescent rapists and sexual-assault offenders as predominately black, lower-class, urban youth. Whether the self-report data would show this profile if they were focused only on violent rapes and sexual assaults remains open to question.

Although we do not deny the value or utility of arrest profiles for certain purposes, they have been used inappropriately to characterize all youthful rapists and sexual-assault offenders. Our understanding of the distribution of rape and sexual assault among youth is not well served by using data that reflect only those officially caught for engaging in these behaviors.

Notes

1. Since sexual assault is a relatively rare behavior, at least in comparison to most other offenses, the number of sexual-assault cases in the sample is rather small. Thus, the sampling error may be large relative to the estimated proportions and means. As a result, it is better to focus on the confidence interval around each mean or proportion because it depicts the range in which the actual values are likely to fall.

2. The results from a series of 2 × 2 chi-square tests (race by sexual-assault offender status) essentially confirmed the t-test results.

3. We did not use the NCS data in this comparison because they do not lend themselves to profiling youthful offenders, for several reasons. First, the NCS data relevant to offenders are derived from victim observations. Therefore nonvisible offender attributes such as social class and place of residence cannot be reported. Second, although victims do report their perceptions of the offender's age and race, these data are not published in a cross-classified form such that the racial distribution of adolescent offenders could be analyzed. Hence, although the NCS can tell what proportion of reported rapes were thought to be committed by adolescents, no other social-correlate data on these youthful offenders are available.

4. Although it would have been desirable to limit this comparison to those youth who committed sexual assaults most akin to forcible rape, the number of such cases was too small to permit a reliable comparison.

5. For some comparisons, the manner in which the data are presented does not permit exclusion of youth ten years of age or younger; however, this group is likely to have little influence on the analyses because they compose less than .005 percent of the under-eighteen group. Also we were not able to discard the females arrested for forcible rape. Their influence is minimal, however, since they constitute less than 1 percent of all individuals arrested for rape.

8
The Sexual-Assault Experience from the Offender's Perspective

The findings concerning the offender's description of the assault and his reactions to it are based on sixty-eight sexual assaults reported by adolescent males for the period 1978 through 1980.[1] As with the victim data, we have chosen generally to summarize across years rather than to present each year separately. In the case of the offender data, this was deemed particularly necessary given the small number of cases in any one year. So that the summarization does not obscure important between- and within-year differences, where they occur they will be noted and discussed.

The assault experiences described represent the most-recent sexual assault reported by each offender in each year. This approach was selected because it was not possible to gather detailed information on all of the assaults reported and because we wanted a constant point of reference for all of the assaults described. Although this approach may improve the accuracy of the information reported because it entails the shortest recall period, it does not necessarily provide a representative description of all sexual assaults committed by adolescent males for the period 1978 through 1980. Since over half of the offenders in each year reported more than one assault, it is possible that data on all of the assaults would provide a different picture from the one offered here. To the extent that the most-recent assault is typical of the others for all offenders, the findings here are representative.

Circumstances of a Sexual Assault

Sexual assaults that are planned ahead of time seem to be rare among this sample of teenage offenders; 70 percent or more of the assaults in each year were either spontaneous or had been thought of only briefly before they occurred. Most adolescent male offenders seemed to be responding to a situation, usually a date, that afforded an opportunity to pursue sexual interests.

Most sexual assaults committed by adolescent males occur in one of three settings: their own homes, their victims' homes, or in an automobile. The proportion of assaults that took place in the home of the victim rose from 25 percent in 1978 to approximately 50 percent in both 1979 and 1980. A decline in the proportion of assaults that occurred in automobiles (from one-third in 1978 to less than 10 percent in 1980) was compensated by a rise in the proportion that occurred out of doors. In no instance did any offenders report that they had picked up their victim while she was hitchhiking. Overall the most-typical setting appears to be the home of the victim.

Of all the sexual assaults described, only eight involved more than one offender. Half of these occurred in 1979. In the majority of these instances of multiple offenders, there were three or four males involved. Typically, however, the offenders reported that they were the only person involved in committing the sexual assault.

To learn about the types of force and pressure used by the offender during the assault, each offender was asked to indicate whether he had employed any of eleven specific types, ranging from verbal persuasion and threats all the way to physical beating, choking, and injury by a weapon (see appendix C for the actual wording of each type). Table 8–1 summarizes the findings from this line of questioning by presenting the proportion of offenders from each year who reported using each type of force or pressure.

According to the offender reports, the primary type of pressure applied was verbal. From 68 percent to 83 percent of the offenders in each year mentioned using this type of pressure. Taking the victim by surprise or causing her to become inebriated or high on drugs were the next most frequently used types. Less than 15 percent of the offenders in any one year indicated that they had used any kind of physical force or weapon in the assault.

Table 8–1
Proportion of Offenders Reporting Use of Each Type of Force, 1978–1980

Type of Force	1978	1979	1980
A. Verbal persuasion	68 (1)	83 (1)	71 (1)
B. Verbal threats of blackmail	7	13	6
C. Verbal threats of injury		9	6
D. Size and strength of offender intimidates	4	9	12
E. Number of offenders intimidates	11 (3)	17	6
F. Victim was drugged or gotten drunk	18 (2)	22 (3)	18 (3)
G. Victim was taken by surprise	7	26 (2)	29 (2)
H. Pushing, slapping, mild roughness	7	9	12
I. Display of a weapon	4		
J. Physical beating and/or choking		4	
K. Injury from a weapon			

Notes: Each offender could report as many types of force as he used. Hence the percentages will not add to one hundred because each offender may be included more than once; however, we have missing data for one offender in 1978 and two in 1980.

The rankings within year for the three most-common types of force reported are in parentheses.

In general, the data from table 8–1 do not suggest any kind of trend with regard to the types of force and pressure used by adolescent males in sexual assaults. There is a clear increase in the proportion of offenders using surprise as a tactic in the assault and in the proportion who perceive that their size and strength intimidated the victim. However, most of the other types of force and pressure do not change substantially over the three years, or peak in 1979 and then decline in 1980.

Table 8–2 synthesizes the data just presented by combining the individual types of force and pressure into four general categories: verbal, situational, threat, and physical. These are loosely ranked from the least to the most serious. Offenders are represented in this table only by the most-serious kind of force they report. Hence a report of both threats and physical force will be recorded in table 8–2 under the physical force only as that was the most-serious kind.

In general, the data in table 8–2 confirm that no trend or pattern is apparent with regard to the type of force used. These data indicate that the proportion of offenders reporting verbal and situational force as the most serious they employed remained fairly stable over the three years examined. The proportion using threats peaked in 1979 and declined dramatically in 1980. The visible increase in the proportion of offenders who resort to physical force (almost twice as many in 1980 as in 1978) is primarily the function of a rise in the number of offenders who reported some pushing, slapping, and mild roughness. It does not reflect an increase in more-violent behavior or the use of weapons. These data indicate that the dominant type of force or pressure used is verbal pressure, although these findings suggest that the proportion of offenders resorting to some physical force is rising.

Comparable to the set of questions asked of the victims, all offenders were asked to respond to a list of factors that could have influenced the sexual assault (see appendix C). The factors ranged from offender and victim characteristics and behavior to situational factors such as time of day or location. Across the three years, the precipitating factors that were

Table 8–2
Proportion of Offenders Who Reported Each Type of Force as the Most Serious They Used, 1978–1980

Type of Force[a]	1978 (N = 28)	1979 (N = 23)	1980 (N = 17)
Verbal (items A and/or B)	50	44	47
Situational (items F and/or G)	21	22	24
Threats (items C, D, E, and/or I)	18	22	6
Physical force (items H, J, and/or K)	7	13	12
Missing data	4		12

[a]See table 8–1 for a listing of the items in each type of force.

consistently cited by 40 percent or more of the offenders were the victim's physical build, the victim's teasing and flirting, and the offender's being sexually excited. Other precipitating factors mentioned by a large proportion in one year or another were the time of day, the victim's being sexually excited, and the type of activity the victim or offender was engaged in. In contrast to the victims who acknowledged little responsibility for the sexual assault, a sizable proportion of the offenders in every year but 1980 indicated that their sexual excitement was a precipitating factor in the sexual assault. From the offender's perspective, a combination of his behavior and that of the victim was responsible for the occurrence of the sexual assault.

In addition to the precipitation questions, the offenders were asked about drinking or taking drugs prior to the assault. An increasing proportion across the three years indicated that they had engaged in one or both of these behaviors (46 percent in 1978, 52 percent in 1979, and 65 percent in 1980). Of this group, from 64 percent to 83 percent indicated that they were drunk or high during the assault. While the offenders themselves do not perceive their drinking or drug taking as instrumental to the sexual assault (less than one-quarter mentioned this when asked about precipitating factors), the potential of these substances to release inhibitions is well known.

When queried about whether the sexual assault had been completed, the proportion of offenders who responded affirmatively varied substantially across the three years: 39 percent answered yes in 1978, 70 percent did in 1979, and 59 percent in 1980. In each of the three years, the primary reason offered for not completing an assault was victim resistance. The only other explanation for failure cited by more than 20 percent of the offenders was their own guilt or fright. Interestingly this response was given by almost 40 percent of the offenders in 1978, but it was not mentioned by any offenders in either of the other two years.

Victim Characteristics

With rare exception (one of which involved both a male and female victim), all of the cases involved a lone, female victim. In over 85 percent of the cases in each year, the offender knew the victim; however, the proportion of known victims declined from 1978 to 1980 such that the highest proportion of victims who were strangers occurred in the last year of the study. For those offenders who said they knew their victim, most indicated she was a date or a girlfriend. Not surprisingly, all or the majority of the victims in each year were adolescents. As would be expected, the ages of the victims increased as the offenders themselves got older. The proportion of victims who were twenty years of age or older grew from zero in 1978 to 30 percent in 1980.

Reactions to a Sexual Assault

In order to learn about reactions to the sexual assault, each offender was asked to respond to a set of adjectives describing his feelings after the assault. Each offender was asked if he felt proud, embarrassed, satisfied, powerful, guilty, and/or confused. The ranking of responses according to the largest proportion responding yes varied only slightly across the years. The two feelings reported consistently by the largest proportion of offenders were satisfied and confused, in that order. In one year or another, other feelings reported by one-third or more of the offenders were pride and guilt. There was great variability across years in the responses, however, as evidenced by the fact that while only 7 percent of the offenders felt proud after the assault in 1978, 39 percent expressed this feeling in 1979. All of the feelings with the exception of confused were reported by a larger proportion of offenders in 1980 than in 1978, though the increase was not always linear across the three-year period. A relatively small proportion of offenders in each year reported feeling embarrassed or powerful.

In addition to their own feelings, the offenders were asked about the reactions of their friends who knew about the sexual assault. First, 40 percent or more of the offenders in each year indicated that their friends knew about the sexual assault. Among the friends who knew, the reaction was overwhelmingly one of approval. Less than 20 percent of the friends in any one year expressed disapproval, while one-quarter or less did not react one way or the other upon hearing about the sexual assault. In general, it appears that the offenders receive strong peer support for their sexually assaultive behavior from their friends who knew about the incident.

Summary

In reviewing these descriptive data, it is important to recall that they are reflective only of the most-recent event reported in each year. To the extent that this event is typical of all sexual assaults committed by each offender, these data may be generalized to all assaults reported for 1978 through 1980. Caution should be exercised in drawing this conclusion, however.

In summarizing the descriptive data provided by the adolescent offenders, the following profile of sexual assault emerges. Most sexual assaults committed by adolescent males are spontaneous events that occur in the context of a date. Little or no planning precedes these incidents. The typical setting for a sexual assault is the offender's or victim's house. A lesser proportion of assaults occur in automobiles.

Offenders view their own sexual excitement and the behavior and physical appearance of the victim as instrumental in causing the assault. Although few of the offenders cited their own drinking or drug taking as a precipitating factor in the assault, a high proportion acknowledged that this behavior occurred prior to the assault. Well over half of those who had been drinking or taking drugs indicated that they were drunk and/or high when the assault occurred.

The primary force or pressure employed in these sexual assaults was verbal. A majority of offenders in each year reported trying to talk their victim into some type of sexual behavior. Only a small proportion of offenders reported using physical force, although there is some evidence that use of this type of force increased from 1978 through 1980. Few assaults involved weapons or more than one offender. In two of the three years, more than half of the sexual assaults were completed according to the offender reports.

In almost all cases, the victim was the girlfriend or the date of the offender. As the offenders matured, the proportion of victims who were strangers increased; however, victims unknown to the offender never constituted more than 12 percent of the sample in any one year. Both offender and victim were adolescents in the majority of cases.

The offenders' reactions to the sexual assault reflect their ambiguity about this experience. The feelings reported by the largest proportion of them include satisfied, confused, guilty, and proud. Reactions of friends who knew about the sexual assault were almost completely approving. Offenders appear to receive strong peer support from their friends for their sexually aggressive behavior.

Overall the picture of sexual assault provided by these adolescent offenders is one of date rape. Little in these data suggest that adolescent sexual assault typically or frequently involves much physical violence or multiple offenders. A more-common situation would be a drunk or high teenage male attempting verbally to pressure or manipulate his date into having sex with him. Support for this sexually aggressive behavior appears to be strong among peers of the offender.

This depiction of adolescent sexual assault could encompass almost all teenage males. Most of them are sexually active, with 80 percent having had sexual intercourse while in their teens (Alan Guttmacher Institute 1981). If we believe contemporary research on dating behavior (Zellman et al. 1981; Koss 1981), a considerable amount of force is associated with demands for sex within the dating context. If this is so, what, if anything, distinguishes the sexual-assault offender from his nonoffending peer who presumably is equally sexually active?

Note

1. This sample of sixty-eight cases is slightly smaller than that used in the prevalence estimates because cases where the respondent refused to answer the sexual-assault questions ($N = 2$) or where the interviewer forgot to ask these questions ($N = 3$) are included in the prevalence estimates but cannot be included here.

9 Prediction of Adolescent Sexual-Assault Offenders

Although the research and literature abound with myths and ideas about the factors that may provoke a sexual assault or incite someone to commit such an act, little effort has been directed toward developing theoretical models to account for the occurrence of sexual assault. In an effort to explain adolescent sexual assault, this chapter proposes and tests an exploratory theoretical model derived from delinquency theory.

Since sexual assault is a delinquent and illegal act, there is a basis for arguing that delinquency theory may be relevant, at least as a framework within which to begin to understand sexually assaultive behavior; however, the sexual component of sexual assault distinguishes it somewhat from other types of physical assaults. Thus we anticipate that a general delinquency theory might not be adequate without some modifications. Therefore we propose to revise a contemporary, integrated theory of delinquent behavior in an attempt to account for sexually assaultive behavior.

Sexual-Assault Model

The underlying conceptual framework for this model is derived from an integrated paradigm of social-control, strain, and social-learning theories developed to account for delinquent behavior (Elliott, Huizinga, and Ageton 1982). The central argument is that to be able to undertake a delinquent act, one must not only be free from (or at least have neutralized) the constraints of conventional values and goals but also have support for the performance of delinquent acts (if they are to persist). One arrives at this position in a number of ways. First, the delinquency paradigm assumes that youth have different early socialization experiences, which result in variable degrees of commitment and integration to the conventional social order. The amount of success or failure (real or anticipated) in achieving conventional goals also may influence one's bonding to society, as may the amount of social disorganization in one's environment. Whether youth actually engage in delinquent acts (and what kind) depends on several factors, but weak bonds to society or the attentuation of initially strong bonds is a necessary (but not sufficient) condition for involvement in delinquent behavior (Elliott and Voss 1974; Elliott, Ageton, and Canter 1979; Elliott, Huizinga, and Ageton 1982).

The model also proposes that access to and involvement in delinquent learning and performance structures is a necessary (but not sufficient) variable in the etiology of delinquent behavior. Delinquent behavior is viewed as meaningful social action; it is behavior that has social meaning and must be supported and rewarded by social groups if it is to continue (Sutherland 1947; Cloward and Ohlin 1960). Most social groups to which an adolescent is exposed such as the family, school, and church are viewed generally as conventional in their normative orientations and the types of behavior modeled and reinforced. The one exception is the peer group, which is typically considered the primary deviant learning context. Thus exposure and commitment to peers involved in delinquent behavior are seen as critical variables in explaining delinquency.

Aside from the relevance of the peer-support variables to a general delinquency model, these variables may have special importance in a study of sexual-assault offenders. Adolescent sexual norms generally are established by peers. Male peer groups that place special emphasis on sexual prowess may encourage sexual aggressiveness among their members; in fact, there is some research that supports this association. In a study of 400 male college students (Kanin 1967b), sexually aggressive males reported that their friends exerted a great deal of pressure for premarital sexual experiences. This pressure was significantly higher than that reported by males who were not sexually aggressive. Furthermore, case studies of adolescent rapists reinforce this finding with descriptions of the pressure these youthful offenders feel from their peers to display sexual prowess (Blanchard 1959). Finally, as Polk and his colleagues noted (1981:388), "Whether or not a male engages in sexually aggressive behavior may be in part a function of the values and expectations of his male friends." Thus, involvement in and commitment to a delinquent peer group that emphasizes masculinity and rewards sexual aggression may be important in the explanation of adolescent sexual assault.

According to the integrated theory, youth who display weak bonds to society or whose initially strong bonds have been reduced and who also belong and are committed to a delinquent peer group are predisposed to some involvement in delinquency. Whether this delinquency takes the form of sexual assault may depend on the presence or absence of several other variables. We have expanded the model to include several variables that our own thinking and previous research on sexual assault suggest may be relevant. The first of these is Attitudes toward Sex Roles.

The emergence of the women's movement in the 1960s initiated a reevaluation of sex roles and their effects on attitudes and behavior. Friedan

(1963), Millett (1970), Chafetz (1974), Rich (1976), and others described the pervasiveness and power of socialization processes that teach girls to be passive, dependent, and subordinate while boys are taught and expected to be strong, dominant, and aggressive. Despite pressure for change from feminists and other forces, studies continue to show that the sex-role conceptions of most men and women are still quite traditional and that these sex roles have important effects on how men and women behave (Broverman et al. 1972; Weitzman 1975).

Griffin (1971) and Brownmiller (1975) among others have argued that the general acceptance, by both men and women, of a dominant, aggressive male posture permits men to assault women (both sexually and otherwise) within the confines of the conventional sex-role definitions. Inasmuch as the conventional female stereotype is passive and dependent, the two sex-role definitions set the stage for acts of male aggression and female acquiescence. If additionally the male oversubscribes to the masculine role image, he may express his aggression through sexual violence in an effort to validate his image by intimidating and dominating the female.

Against this culture backdrop, teenage males whose sexuality is just emerging may feel great pressure, especially from peers, to demonstrate their masculinity by performing sexually. The degree to which an adolescent male and his peers subscribe to traditional sex-role stereotypes may influence the commission of sexual assaults. We expect that sexual-assault offenders will evidence a strong adherence to conventional sex-role conceptions. We are not arguing, however, that this factor by itself could produce an assault but only that it provides an attitudinal framework supportive of such an act.

The second variable we have added, Involvement in Assaultive Behavior, is derived from research using official arrest records that suggests that men who engage in sexual assault also engage in other physically assaultive behaviors (Amir 1967; Wolfgang 1958; MacDonald 1971). Research findings from these studies show that from 20 percent to 43 percent of those arrested for rape and sexual assault had previous arrest records for other offenses against the person. Social class has been offered by some, most notably Marvin Wolfgang, as the explanation for these findings. Wolfgang argues that there is a subculture of violence that is pervasive within the lower classes and accounts for the disproportionate number of lower-class offenders charged with violent crimes of all types (Wolfgang and Ferracuti 1967). Despite the fact that this finding is based on arrest records, it has been used to argue for a direct relationship between the commission of sexual assault and social class (Brownmiller 1975).

Although a reasonable amount of research suggests that violent behavior (not arrests for such) is fairly evenly distributed in the population by social class (Martin 1976; Fotjik 1976; Pizzey 1974), official data and, to a large extent, public opinion continue to argue for a class association. Given this situation, we decided to include both social class and a measure of involvement in assaultive behavior as variables in our sexual-assault model. We expect that social class will not be associated with sexual assault and that involvement in assaultive behavior may be related to sexual assault if other critical factors are present.

Finally, delinquency research on neutralization and rationalization of antisocial behavior has led us to include some variables related to these processes. Researchers in this area (Matza 1964; Cressey 1953; Sykes and Matza 1957; Scott and Lyman 1968) have long argued that conventionally socialized individuals who commit deviant acts use various techniques to release themselves from the guilt and inhibitions they may feel. These techniques such as dehumanizing potential victims, denying that injury occurred, or arguing that the victim deserved what she or he got allow offenders to perpetrate antisocial acts by overcoming learned inhibitions and avoiding guilt or remorse. In a study of victim stereotypes (Schwendinger and Schwendinger 1967), it was observed that delinquents implicitly defined the victim as a worthless human being. Data from this study reinforce the assumption that delinquents tacitly hold a common attitude toward victims based on stereotypic definitions and images. With regard to the crime of rape, it has been argued that defining the victim as consenting and willing both evokes less moral resistance to the act and reduces feelings of guilt (Fattah 1976). Overall, the extent to which an individual uses such techniques or adheres to attitudes that accommodate these rationalizations, the more he may be able to justify deviant behavior.

Focusing specifically on rape and sexual assault, some research findings suggest the kind of attitudinal structures that could release inhibitions prior to a sexual assault and reduce guilt afterward. Research on rape myths has demonstrated that conventional beliefs about rape are systematically related to other cultural attitudes such as sex-role stereotyping, adversarial sexual beliefs, and acceptance of interpersonal violence (Burt 1980).[1] Although this research was not directed to exploring the relationship between these attitudes and the commission of sexual assault, such a connection seems implicit. In fact, research findings have demonstrated that offenders' perceptions of rape are likely to play a key role in their decision to assault a woman (Abel, Madden, and Christopher 1975). Further, a recent study comparing a group of incarcerated rapists and a group of convicts imprisoned for other crimes indicated that the rapists more frequently endorsed stereotypical beliefs about rape than did the nonrapists (Scully and Marolla 1982).

Accepting the logic and findings from the delinquency research on neutralization and rationalization of antisocial behavior as well as from the work on rape myths has led us to add two measures to our model. Inclusion of the scales Attitudes toward Rape and Sexual Assault and Attitudes toward Interpersonal Violence will allow an exploration of the potential relationship between these attitudes and sexual assault. We anticipate that adolescents who hold stereotypic views of sexual assault and attitudes supportive of interpersonal violence will be more prone to commit sexual assault than their peers who do not adhere to such beliefs.

In summary, youth who display weak bonds to society or whose initially strong bonds have been attenuated and who also belong and are committed to a delinquent peer group are predisposed to involvement in some kind of delinquency. If this delinquency is to take the form of sexual assault, certain other factors are seen as relevant. Peer-group encouragement and rewards for sexually aggressive behavior are central. Also attitudes supportive of interpersonal violence and stereotypic ideas about sexual assault and sex roles increase the likelihood of a sexual assault. The model also suggests that youth who engage in other assaultive behavior may be more prone to commit a sexual assault than those who do not.

It is clear that this is basically a delinquency model and presupposes that a delinquent profile and peer group are associated with the commission of sexual assault. We recognize, however, that the pervasiveness and power of sex-role stereotypes in our society may make it possible for sexual assault to occur outside a delinquent context. Sexual aggression with its strong ties to traditional male role patterns probably is well supported within conventional male peer groups. Consequently isolated or infrequent acts of sexual assault may be committed by basically nondelinquent youth. Nonetheless, the model asserts that a repetitive or sustained pattern of sexual assault requires a delinquent orientation and rewards from a peer group that is supportive of a variety of delinquent behavior, including that which is sexually assaultive.

Analysis Procedures

The initial analyses of our conceptualization are static tests. For each of the three years, we employ t-tests and chi-square tests to compare offenders and nonoffenders on the demographic and theoretical variables proposed in the model. Findings from these analyses will help to establish whether there are any basic demographic, behavioral, or attitudinal differences between the two groups and how consistent these differences are across the study period. In addition, these analyses should reveal something about the power and the consistency of the theoretical variables to differentiate the offenders from the nonoffenders.

Following these analyses, we compare the offenders and controls in 1976 and 1977 on any variables that consistently differentiated the groups in the annual tests. These analyses will allow us to see whether the two groups could be distinguished as much as two years prior to any sexual-assault reports.

Finally, we conduct a series of discriminant analyses to see how well the set of theoretical variables can distinguish the offenders from the non-offenders. These multivariate tests also will provide information on the relative contribution of each variable to the overall discriminant function. Hence, we will be able to determine which of the variables are most powerful in distinguishing between the two groups.

The first step in these analyses was to select a control group for the offenders in each year. The eligible pool in each year was all males with no sexual-assault reports in that year or previously, either as a victim or an offender. This group was stratified by race and class, and a systematic sample of roughly the same size as the male-offender sample in each year was drawn. By stratifying, we were able to ensure that the control groups would be representative of the larger population from which they were drawn, at least with regard to race and social class. As with the victim control groups, statistical comparisons were made between the selected control groups and the male population from which they were drawn on such variables as race, social class, place of residence, and age. For 1978, 1979, and 1980, these tests showed no significant differences between the control group and the larger population on any of the tested variables.

Offender and Control-Group Comparisons, 1978–1980

1978 Comparisons

The analyses involving the sociodemographic variables produced no significant differences by race, social class, age, or place of residence. A significant finding was observed, however, on the number of disruptive events in the home such as divorce, long-term unemployment, and death. The offenders experienced significantly more family crises in 1978 than did the controls ($t = 2.04$, $p \leq .05$).

On the general attitudinal and behavioral measures, several striking differences emerged. The offenders reported significantly more normlessness in all settings: the home, school, and peer group.[2] To a much greater degree than the controls, they seem to feel that achievement or attainment of goals requires unconventional, illegitimate means. A complementary finding was that the controls perceived significantly less negative labeling from parents, peers, and teachers than did the offenders.[3] In all these settings, the offenders think they are viewed less positively than do the nonoffenders.

With regard to peer-group differences between the offenders and nonoffenders, the findings are very consistent (see Table 9–1). In all instances the offenders display significantly more commitment and exposure to delin-

Table 9-1
Significant Mean($\bar{X}$) Differences between Offenders and Nonoffenders on Peer Variables, 1978

Variable	Offender $\bar{X}$	SD	Control $\bar{X}$	SD	t-Value	p
Perceived Peer Disapproval of Delinquent Behavior	36.03	4.50	39.86	6.48	2.67	.01
Perceived Peer Disapproval of Forced Sex	2.76	0.87	3.79	0.56	−5.65	.00
Perceived Peer Disapproval of Sexual Intercourse	2.42	1.03	3.10	0.90	−2.77	.01
Exposure to Delinquent Peers	30.57	6.69	23.09	6.51	4.46	.00
Commitment to Delinquent Peers	5.18	1.74	4.28	1.07	2.50	.05
Involvement with Friends	10.19	2.91	8.31	3.65	−2.13	.05
Peer Normlessness	10.33	2.38	8.90	2.04	−2.56	.01
Perceived Negative Labeling by Peers	26.30	4.31	23.12	4.26	−2.92	.01

quent peers, as well as less disapproval from peers for delinquent and sexually aggressive behavior. Also they are substantially more involved with their friends than are the controls. To a large degree, sexual-assault offenders appear to operate in a peer network that reinforces their delinquent and sexually assaultive behavior.

Given the peer-group differences, it is not surprising that the offenders and controls evidence substantially different levels of involvement in delinquent behavior. On all but one of the delinquency scales (the one exception is drug use), the offenders are significantly more delinquent than the control group. Their attitudinal set with regard to interpersonal violence is also different. The controls are significantly less likely to endorse violent physical behavior than are the offenders ($t = 1.99, p \leq .05$). Finally, the data show that the offenders have experienced significantly more victimization than the controls.

Despite these findings, it is important to note that the two groups were not differentiated on the Attitudes toward Sex Roles or Attitudes toward Rape and Sexual Assault scales. At least in 1978, the offenders do not display stereotypic sex-role and sexual-assault attitudes. We would not have predicted either of these results from the model, but it remains to be seen whether they will confirmed in the data from 1979 and 1980.

Overall the data show no substantial demographic differences between the offenders and controls with the exception of the number of disruptive home events experienced. The findings do indicate that the offender group associates with and is committed to a delinquent peer group, which provides support for sexually aggressive behavior. The offenders also appear more estranged than the controls from conventional settings such as the home and school. Finally, they are clearly more delinquent in general and hold attitudes that facilitate engaging in physically violent or rough behavior.

1979 Comparisons

Of all the sociodemographic variables analyzed, only race showed a significant difference; 44 percent of the offenders were minority-group members compared to only 29 percent of the controls. In all other respects, the two groups were demographically similar.

Table 9–2 displays the attitudinal and behavioral variables that evidence significant differences between the 1979 offenders and nonoffenders. In the family context, these findings suggest that the offenders feel isolated and negatively labeled by their families to a significantly greater degree than do the controls. The data also show that the controls are substantially more involved in and attribute importance to family activities and bonds. Overall these findings are stronger than those in 1978 in suggesting that the offender is estranged from and uninvolved with his family, at least in comparison to the nonoffender.

Within the school context, the results are not as strong as in the home but still suggestive that the offender is not strongly committed to this conventional setting. The scores on both the Academic Aspirations-Current Success and Normlessness scales suggest that the offenders do not feel they are doing well in school and that to do well, they feel they have to break the rules. These findings coupled with those from the home indicate that the sexual-assault offender is not as strongly bonded to either setting as is the nonoffender.

Of all the contexts examined, the peer context shows the strongest and most-consistent differences between the two groups. The controls have significantly less exposure to delinquent peers than do the offenders. The offenders' peer groups provide support for delinquent and sexually aggressive behavior to a far greater degree than those of the nonoffenders. These findings demonstrate that sexual-assault offenders, in contrast to their nonoffending peers, are involved with delinquent friends who endorse and encourage all types of delinquent behavior.

Given these findings, it is not surprising that the two groups have significantly different levels of involvement in delinquency. As the results from table 9–2 show, the offenders report significantly higher frequency scores on several types of delinquent behavior. In addition, they experience substantially more trouble from drinking and drug use than do the controls. There is considerable overlap in the scores, however, indicated by the relatively large standard deviations, especially for the offender group.

In summary, the demographic data suggest a racial disparity between the composition of the offender and control groups, although we did not observe one in the 1978 comparison. A substantially higher proportion of the offenders were minority-group members. Findings from comparisons on

Table 9-2
Significant Mean ($\bar{X}$) Differences between Offenders and Nonoffenders on Attitudinal and Behavioral Scales, 1979

Scale Name	Offender $\bar{X}$	SD	Control $\bar{X}$	SD	t-Value	p
Family variables						
Family Aspirations-						
Current Success	16.38	3.29	19.37	4.53	2.50	.05
Involvement in Family						
Activities	6.76	3.27	9.29	4.03	2.23	.05
Social Isolation from Family	11.30	2.82	9.09	2.50	−2.82	.01
Perceived Negative Labeling						
by Family	30.72	8.17	24.04	4.44	−3.45	.00
Family Normlessness	10.39	2.84	8.57	2.29	−2.40	.05
School variables						
Academic Aspirations-						
Current Success	14.13	4.15	17.31	3.90	2.50	.05
School Normlessness	12.90	2.64	11.00	2.15	−2.54	.05
Peer variables						
Peer Normlessness	10.22	2.17	8.65	1.87	−2.62	.01
Perceived Negative Labeling						
by Peers	27.66	5.94	23.00	3.81	−3.17	.00
Exposure to Delinquent Peers	33.17	8.99	24.71	7.99	−3.37	.00
Perceived Peer Disapproval						
of Delinquent Behavior	33.52	6.28	39.87	5.64	3.61	.00
Perceived Peer Disapproval						
of Sexual Intercourse	2.13	0.87	3.00	1.04	3.07	.00
Perceived Peer Disapproval						
of Forced Sex	2.83	0.98	3.87	0.63	4.29	.00
Peer Pressure for Drinking						
and Drug Use[a]	13.22	4.31	10.52	4.03	−2.19	.05
General variables						
Trouble from Drinking[a]	8.27	2.95	6.15	2.68	−2.44	.05
Trouble from Drug Use[a]	8.22	3.12	5.73	1.27	−3.01	.01
Delinquent behavior						
Felony Assault	2.65	3.50	0.17	0.49	−3.36	.00
Public Disorder	25.48	32.18	6.65	13.63	−2.58	.05
Crimes against Persons	11.30	16.08	2.00	4.42	2.67	.01
General Theft	6.48	10.77	0.96	1.92	−2.42	.05
Index Offenses	4.78	5.30	0.32	0.78	−3.99	.00
Home-related Delinquency	2.52	3.90	0.30	0.70	−2.69	.01

[a]These measures were available for all subjects only in 1979 and 1980.

the attitudinal and behavioral measures show clearly that the offenders are more delinquent and that they receive support and reinforcement for this behavior from their peers. Sexual behavior generally, and sexually aggressive behavior specifically, are endorsed by the offenders' peer groups to a significantly greater degree than by the friends of the nonoffenders. In addition, the offenders' lack of commitment to school and home suggests that there may not be any strong, countervailing forces in their lives to counter the delinquent orientation of their peer groups.

1980 Comparisons

The offender and control groups in 1980 were almost identical demographically. No race, age, social-class, or place-of-residence differences emerged. The only demographic variable that differentiated the groups was the variable Family Crises. The offenders experienced significantly more of these in their families than did the controls ($t = -2.12$, $p. \leq .05$).

On the attitudinal and behavioral variables (see table 9–3), the offender and control groups are differentiated in much the same way as in previous years. The offenders perceive substantially more negative labeling from their family than do the controls. For the first time in 1980, we asked about the work context and discovered that the offenders perceive more negative labeling than the controls in this context as well. The findings on the scale Family Normlessness suggest that the offenders do not feel bound by their parents' moral code. With regard to the family as well as the work place, it appears that the offenders are not nearly as committed or well integrated as are the controls.

The strongest and most-consistent differences between the two groups may be seen in the peer variables once more. The offenders are significantly more exposed and committed to delinquent peers. In addition, their peers are substantially less disapproving of sexual intercourse, forced sex, and delinquent behavior in general than are the peers of the control-groups members. This support for delinquent behavior manifests itself in actual behavior; the offenders are significantly more involved in several kinds of illegal acts than are the controls. There are, however, fewer significant differences in delinquent behavior between the groups in 1980 than in 1979.

Although the offenders and controls are clearly different in terms of the structure and orientation of peer groups and the integration and commitment of families, they do not hold distinctly different attitudes toward sex roles or rape and sexual assault. Furthermore, their views about interpersonal violence are roughly comparable.

General Summary

In summarizing the findings from 1978 through 1980, we have operated with the rule of thumb that significant differences that appear in two or more years are likely to reflect real, substantive distinctions between sexual-assault offenders and nonoffenders. Hence we will confine our comments generally to variables that meet this criterion.

Demographically the only variable that consistently distinguishes the offenders from the nonoffenders is the number of family crises reported. In two of the three years reviewed, the families of the offenders experienced significantly more crises such as divorce and prolonged unemployment than

Table 9-3
Significant Mean ($\bar{X}$) Differences between Offenders and Nonoffenders on Attitudinal and Behavioral Scales, 1980

Scale Name	Offender $\bar{X}$	SD	Control $\bar{X}$	SD	t-Value	p
Family variables						
Family Normlessness	10.76	2.05	9.06	1.82	−2.57	.05
Perceived Negative Labeling by Family	30.35	8.09	25.12	4.79	−2.29	.05
Perceived Negative Labeling by Coworkers	30.69	7.17	24.86	4.24	−2.55	.05
Peer variables						
Peer Normlessness	10.59	2.37	9.00	2.15	−2.04	.05
Perceived Negative Labeling by Peers	28.59	6.10	23.00	3.74	−3.22	.00
Perceived Peer Disapproval of Forced Sex	3.59	0.62	4.24	0.66	2.94	.01
Perceived Peer Disapproval of Sexual Intercourse	2.47	0.72	3.35	1.12	2.74	.01
Perceived Peer Disapproval of Delinquent Behavior	34.94	5.49	41.76	5.39	3.66	.00
Exposure to Delinquent Peers	33.24	9.30	24.47	7.88	−2.96	.01
Commitment to Delinquent Peers	6.00	1.37	4.47	1.59	−3.01	.01
General variables						
Trouble from Drug Use[a]	8.00	3.55	5.11	0.33	−3.13	.01
Delinquent behavior						
Minor Theft	4.47	4.91	0.41	1.23	−3.30	.00
General Theft	8.71	11.13	0.47	1.23	−3.03	.01
Index Offenses	9.12	13.09	0.24	0.56	−2.80	.01

[a]These measures were available for all subjects only in 1979 and 1980.

did those of the controls. Although we have no evidence for a direct association between the commission of sexual assault and a high number of family crises, one could argue, as others have done, that an unstable home environment provides a climate for delinquent behavior generally.

The absence of any significant race, social-class, or place-of-residence differences in these comparisons using behavioral data is in direct contrast to the findings derived from UCR data on adolescent rapists; however, results from other self-report research on rape and sexual assault confirm these findings (Polk et al. 1981; Smithyman 1978; Kanin 1967a). Other factors may differentiate sexual-assault offenders from nonoffenders, but demographically the two groups are nearly identical.

One place where the two groups are consistently different is in their home environment. Aside from experiencing more family crises, the offenders also report significantly higher scores on the scales Family Normlessness and Perceived Negative Labeling by Family. Both of these findings suggest that the offenders do not have a strong attachment to their parents and that they are estranged from their home settings. Some alienation from the school setting is also manifested by the offenders. In two of the three years, the offenders are substantially more inclined than the controls to report that one has to violate school norms and rules in order to achieve academically.

Some of the strongest findings from these analyses are associated with the peer group and involvement in delinquent behavior. For all three years, sexual-assault offenders had a significantly higher exposure to delinquent peers and received support from these friends for unconventional, delinquent acts. In particular, the data indicate that the offenders' peers are substantially less disapproving of sexual intercourse and forced sex than are the peers of the nonoffenders. Furthermore, the offenders themselves were significantly more involved in a wide variety of delinquent behavior, including physical assaults. The offenders also reported significantly more trouble from drug use than did the controls. Although there were fewer significant differences in delinquent behavior between the two groups in 1980 than in 1978, the offenders are still substantially more involved in several types of delinquency than are the controls.

Taken altogether, the findings from these comparisons support some of the variables in the sexual-assault model and dispute others. The general applicability of à model based on delinquency theory seems demonstrated by several of the results. First, the offenders clearly are less integrated and committed to conventional social settings, especially the home and family. The findings are not as strong with regard to the school setting, but the direction is consistent, with the offenders' reporting more estrangement than the controls from this conventional environment as well. Second, their exposure and bonding to delinquent peers is strong and consistent. Furthermore, their peers provide substantially more support for sexually aggressive behavior than do the peers of the nonoffenders. And finally, the offenders are consistently and substantially more delinquent than the nonoffenders. The two groups differ on all types of delinquency, including assaultive behavior, as the model predicted they would.

The data do not conform to the model with regard to the offenders' sex-role and sexual-assault attitudes as well as their attitudes toward interpersonal violence. On all of these scales, the attitudinal set of the offenders is not significantly different from that of the controls. Based on this initial examination, these attitudes do not appear to be as relevant to the commission of sexual assault as the model had proposed.

Pre-Sexual-Assault Comparisons

If offenders and controls can be distinguished after the assault has occurred, one obvious question is whether those differences existed prior to the assault and might in some way account for the different behavior of the two groups.[4] Since we have data on all subjects for two years before the SAP began (for 1976 and 1977), we decided to address this issue at least partially by comparing an offender and control group before they became differentiated by their sexual-assault reports.

The comparison groups consisted of all male offenders in 1978 who had not reported a sexual assault in 1976 or 1977[5] and a group of controls who reported no sexual assaults across the entire study period (1976 through 1980). Using the 1976 and 1977 data, a series of t-tests were conducted to compare these two groups on all of the available theoretical variables as well as the self-report delinquency scales.[6] Table 9-4 displays the mean differences between these two groups for the years 1976 and 1977 on the scales that significantly differentiated the groups.

In 1976, the future sexual-assault offenders and the controls do not appear substantially different, although the differences that are present are in the predicted direction. The offenders-to-be are significantly more tolerant of deviant behavior than the controls and have a peer group that is more approving of delinquent behavior than the peers of the control group. The findings also indicate that two years prior to their sexual-assault reports, the future offenders are substantially more committed to a delinquent peer group than are the controls. In addition, the controls are better integrated into the home and family, as evidenced by the significant difference between they and the offenders-to-be on the Family Normlessness scale. Finally, although none of the delinquency scales evidence significant differences between the groups, the offenders-to-be report higher frequency scores in all instances.

When the two groups are compared one year prior to the first reports of sexual assault (in 1977), the pattern of differences observed in the 1976 data is strengthened. The future offenders are still less well bonded to the family than are the controls. Not only are the two groups significantly different on the Family Normlessness scale, as in 1976, but the controls report substantially less negative labeling by their parents than do the future offenders. In addition, the groups are significantly different in their perceptions of negative labeling by teachers, with the future offenders perceiving substantially more than the controls. Taken together, all of these findings suggest that the offenders-to-be are not as well bonded as the controls to the two primary conventional settings in the lives of adolescents, the home and the school.

With regard to the peer variables, the 1977 findings generally reinforce and strengthen the 1976 differences. The future offenders continue to show significantly more approval from peers for delinquent behavior and now are reporting substantially more exposure to delinquent peers as well. Furthermore, a significant difference between the groups on the scale Peer Normlessness indicates the future offenders' low commitment to conventional social norms. Although the 1977 data no longer evidence a significant difference between the groups on commitment to delinquent peers, the future offenders clearly are more aligned with a delinquent peer network than are the controls.

Table 9-4
Mean Differences between Future Sexual-Assault Offenders (O) and Controls (C) on Selected Attitudinal Scales

Scale Name	1976 O	SD	C	SD	t-Value	p	1977 O	SD	C	SD	t-Value	p
Family and school variables												
Family Normlesssness	10.00	2.34	8.72	2.09	2.35	.05	9.99	2.14	8.79	2.13	2.23	.05
Perceived Negative Labeling by Family	28.04	6.51	26.81	4.92	0.83	NS	25.26	4.34	23.20	3.05	2.12	.05
Perceived Negative Labeling by Teachers	27.67	5.78	26.94	3.83	0.57	NS	28.06	5.60	22.44	2.97	2.19	.05
Peer variables												
Perceived Peer Disapproval of Delinquent Behavior	32.81	5.52	35.42	4.35	−2.04	.05	31.67	4.74	34.28	3.90	−2.35	.05
Exposure to Delinquent Peers	19.71	8.51	16.96	5.76	1.30	NS	21.72	6.67	17.84	5.75	2.37	.05
Commitment to Delinquent Peers	4.86	1.91	3.81	1.06	2.29	.05	4.56	1.40	4.18	1.24	1.09	NS
Peer Normlessness	10.10	2.08	9.18	1.96	1.81	NS	13.18	1.98	11.10	2.40	3.81	.00
General variables												
Attitudes toward Deviance	28.67	4.89	31.24	3.68	−2.32	.05	27.84	5.17	29.41	4.17	−1.31	NS

Note: The offender group is composed of all offenders who reported a sexual assault for the first time in the study in 1978 and had participated in the study in both 1976 and 1977 ($N = 27$). The control group is composed of the wave 4 and 5 control who had participated in the study in 1976 and 1977 ($N = 39$). We combined the two to increase the N after discovering that none of the wave 4 controls reported a sexual assault in wave 5.

The frequency of involvement in all types of delinquency is higher for the future offenders than for the controls in 1977. While the mean differences on several of the delinquency scales are substantial, the variances are also large, thus precluding significant findings.

To summarize, the data from 1976 and 1977 suggest that even before committing any sexual assaults, the offender group could be distinguished from the controls on several key theoretical variables. Most specifically, the offenders are not as well bonded to the home or school as are the non-offenders. In both of these contexts, the offender group reports significantly more negative labeling by parents and teachers, which is indicative of low integration and commitment to these settings. Further evidence of low bonding to the home on the part of the offenders is found in the Family Normlessness scores. In both years, the controls report significantly lower scores than do the offenders, implying a stronger commitment to or belief in the value structures of the family. Although the offenders do not report substantially different scores from the controls on other measures reflecting estrangement from home and school, the general pattern of scores on all of the bonding variables suggests they are less integrated and committed to these contexts.

The 1976 and 1977 pattern of scores on the peer variables demonstrates that as much as one to two years prior to their reported assault, the offenders were more involved in and committed to delinquent peer groups than were the controls. These groups consistently were less disapproving of delinquent behavior than the peer groups of the controls. Clearly the offenders were enmeshed in a delinquent peer network to a significantly greater degree than the controls as much as two years before any reported sexual assaults.

Although the offenders report higher frequency scores on all of the delinquency scales in both 1976 and 1977, their involvement in delinquency is not consistently and significantly different from that of the controls. Not until 1978 when the first sexual assaults are reported do the two groups really become distinct in terms of most of the delinquency scales.

Overall these analyses suggest that some of the factors that separated the offenders and controls after or simultaneously with the report of a sexual assault were present as much as two years prior. The differences between the groups, however, were not nearly as strong or consistent as they were after the first reported sexual assaults. How influential these variables were in causing the sexual assaults remains to be seen, for we have yet to conduct a multivariate analysis with the variables in the proper temporal order to predict sexually assaultive behavior.

Multivariate Assessment of the Integrated Delinquency Model

Although we have argued that the explanation of delinquency is well defined by the integrated delinquency theory, we have presented no empirical evidence to support this position. Since our argument about the basic relevance of this theory to the prediction of sexual assault is predicated on the theory's applicability for delinquency generally, we felt it important to document the validity of this model.

A detailed test of the integrated theoretical delinquency model is presented in Elliott, Huizinga, and Ageton (1982). Using a path-analysis approach, the model was used to predict several types of delinquency, including general delinquency, serious index offenses, minor offenses, marijuana use, and hard-drug use. Two independent tests of the model were undertaken, using one-year lagged independent and dependent variables. The initial analysis used data from 1976 and 1977, and this analysis was independently replicated using data from 1977 to 1978. Although the model was tested on the full NYS sample and by sex, we will confine our comments to the results for males since they are the group of interest to us with regard to sexual assault.

For the males, the model accounted for 54 to 58 percent of the variance in general delinquent behavior. When the criterion measure involved serious delinquent acts, the level of explained variance was smaller but still substantial (36 to 37 percent). The variance explained for the remaining types of delinquency for all males is as follows: minor offenses, 41 to 45 percent; marijuana use, 62 percent; and hard-drug use, 34 to 50 percent. The primary factors influencing delinquent behavior and drug use were prior delinquency and involvement in delinquent peer groups.

Overall the explanatory power of the integrated model for males is quite good, given the level of prediction currently reported in the delinquency and drug-use literature. Further, the relative consistency in the initial and replication findings increases our confidence in these estimates of the model's explanatory power.

Test of the Sexual-Assault Model

To test the sexual-assault model, we conducted a discriminant analysis in order to assess the power of the variables to discriminate between the sexual-assault offenders and the controls. This analysis assesses the ability of multiple variables to distinguish between two or more groups.

Drawing on the experience of the empirical efforts by Elliott, Huizinga, and Ageton (1982), we selected basically the same set of independent variables used in that work. In addition, we added the specific measures thought to be associated with sexual assault.

The strain measures reflect the discrepancy between a subject's aspirations and the perceived actual achievement relative to his aspirations in the home and school contexts. A high score on the strain measures indicates a high perceived discrepancy between personal aspirations and goals, and present achievement.

Four scales assess bonding to the conventional social order. The Family and School Involvement scales assess the amount of time spent with the family and on academic concerns. These scales reflect participation in conventional settings and activities, and a high score indicates heavy involvement. The Normlessness scales assess a subject's commitment to conventional social norms at home and at school. Conceptually normlessness refers to the belief that one must violate the rules and norms to achieve personal goals or aspirations. A high score reflects a strong commitment to the conventional norms at home or school.

Integration into a delinquent peer group is measured by joint consideration of the involvement or time spent with peers and the delinquent or conventional orientation of the peer group. It is a constructed measure combining time spent with peers and the delinquent or nondelinquent orientation of the peer group.[7] A high positive score implies strong bonding to a delinquent peer group.

Among the specific variables added to make the model more relevant to sexual assault are Attitudes toward Rape and Sexual Assault, Sex-Role Attitudes, Attitudes toward Interpersonal Violence, Perceived Peer Disapproval for Sexual Intercourse, and Forced Sex and Crimes against Persons (a measure of involvement in all assaultive behaviors). (See appendix A.)

Within the set, some variables provide point estimates (estimates that reflect attitudes or aspirations at the time of the interview such as Attitudes toward Sex Roles) and others provide interval estimates (estimates that cover the period of the calendar year prior to the interview such as Crimes against Persons). The time location of the measures is important since our predictive capability is strengthened when the temporal order is controlled in the analysis. Given both point and interval estimates and the causal linkages among the integrated delinquency variables, we could not always ensure the correct temporal ordering without a very long time lag.[8] What we were able to do, however, was ensure that all of the point-estimate independent variables were temporally prior and that the interval-estimate variables were simultaneous with a report of sexual assault (or nonreport for the controls). Hence the variables we are using to discriminate the offenders from nonoffenders encompass the same year interval as the assault report or are temporally prior.

Initially we proposed to include all of the male offenders (1978 through 1980) and controls in the discriminant analysis; however, because we did not gather data on all the specific sexual-assault variables until the 1978 survey, we could not include the offenders who reported in 1978 and still maintain the proper temporal order for these variables. For example, an offender who reported a sexual assault in 1978 would have no score on Attitudes toward Sex Roles preceding his sexual-assault report because this variable was not in the survey until 1978. Thus we tested the model with just the 1979 and 1980 offenders and controls since they would have all the original theoretical variables as well as the added sexual-assault ones in the proper sequence. A stepwise procedure was used so that the order in which the independent variables were examined was the order of their discriminating power. This procedure provides data on the contribution of each variable in the model to the discrimination of the groups.

Among the variables analyzed, only four were needed to define the discriminant function. The variables that contributed to the classification of the groups in order of importance were Involvement with Delinquent Peers, Crimes against Persons (a measure of involvement in assaultive behavior), Attitudes toward Rape and Sexual Assault, and Family Normlessness. None of the other variables made a sizable enough contribution in the presence of the four discriminating variables to influence the discriminant function.

Of the four discriminating variables, two are from the integrated delinquency model, including the variable that makes the strongest contribution to the discriminant function: Involvement with Delinquent Peers. This finding reinforces the general appropriateness of analyzing sexual-assault offenders within a delinquency framework. However, some discriminating power is added by the rape attitudes and involvement in assaultive-behavior scales.

Overall the combined power of the four variables correctly classified 77 percent of all the cases; however, one-third of the offenders and almost 20 percent of the controls were incorrectly identified in this analysis. Thus although the overall rate of correct assignment is reasonably high, the level of incorrect classification within groups is relatively large. Furthermore, Wilks Lambda, a statistic that measures group mean differences over several variables, was .68, indicating only moderate separation between the offender and nonoffender groups. While the sexual-assault model does have some ability to discriminate between the groups, it is not sufficient to achieve a high level of accuracy.

Although we had believed that the integrated delinquency model was not sufficient to explain sexually assaultive behavior, the findings led us to rethink this position. The fact that so few of the added variables (two out of six) contributed to the discrimination of the groups suggested that they might not be as important as we previously had thought. Consequently we decided to conduct a second discriminant analysis using just the variables from the integrated delinquency model. A comparison between this analysis and the one just described would allow us to judge which model provided better discrimination between sexual-assault offenders and controls.

When the discriminant analysis was run with just the delinquency variables, only one variable provided any discriminatory power between the offender and control groups. Involvement with Delinquent Peers by itself correctly classified 76 percent of the cases, with incorrect assignment of about one-third of the offender cases and 20 percent of the control cases.

The separation between the groups was still only fair, as evidenced by a Wilks Lambda of .78.

The accuracy of the classification with the delinquency model, in fact with only one variable from that model, is almost the same as that with the sexual-assault model. Clearly the additional sexual-assault variables offer little improvement to the accuracy of the classification over that achieved with just one variable from the delinquency model. Furthermore, as the variable Involvement with Delinquent Peers entered first in both the discriminant analyses, it is clear that it is a central factor in distinguishing offenders from nonoffenders. This is not an unexpected result because the test of the integrated model with the full NYS male sample singled out this variable as the best predictor.

Overall if we were to consider just the discriminant analysis findings, we might conclude that even the full delinquency model is not necessary because only the variable Involvement with Delinquent Peers made any contribution to the final discriminant function. If, however, we consider these findings in conjunction with those from the offender and control comparisons, both before and after the reported sexual assaults, the full delinquency model does appear to be relevant. All of the results point to the fact that sexual-assault offenders are basically delinquent youth. They are not well integrated into the conventional social order and report strong bonds to delinquent peers. In the annual comparisons, the offenders and controls consistently showed significant differences on peer, home, and school variables, with the offenders always reporting more involvement with delinquent peers and more estrangement from school and home. Several of these differences were noted as much as two years prior to the first reported assaults. Also the offenders were substantially more involved in several types of delinquent behavior across all three years. The importance of associating with a delinquent peer group was reinforced by the discriminant analyses.

The idea that sexual-assault offenders are influenced strongly by stereotypic views of rape and sexual assault, traditional sex-role attitudes, and liberal beliefs about the use of violence was not borne out in these analyses. None of these variables consistently differentiated the offenders and nonoffenders in the annual comparisons. Furthermore, in the initial discriminant analyses, only the measure of rape attitudes contributed to the separation of the groups. Clearly it is not a critical factor, however, since its absence in the discriminant analysis involving just delinquency variables had little effect on the accuracy of the classification. Although we do not deny that the constellation of beliefs about male and female roles, behavior, and sexuality may influence sexual acts, the data do not indicate that such attitudes play a major role in predicting sexual assault.

One place where the initial discriminant analysis and the annual comparisons differ is with regard to the role of peer disapproval for sexual intercourse and forced sex. While the offenders do report significantly less disapproval in their peer networks for these behaviors (see tables 9–1, 9–2, and 9–3), this difference did not play a role in distinguishing one group from the other in the first discriminant analysis. This is not surprising, however, given the power of the measure Involvement with Delinquent Peers. The stepwise discriminant statistics indicate that almost all of the discriminating power of the variables Peer Disapproval of Sexual Intercourse and Forced Sex is captured by Involvement with Delinquent Peers. Since this last variable is the first to enter the discriminant analysis, it effectively eliminates any separate contribution the peer-support variables might make.

To summarize, we feel that all of the results in concert indicate that sexual-assault offenders are basically delinquent youth and that sexually assaultive behavior is explained fairly well by the integrated delinquency model. The findings are inconsistent as to the importance of the added sexual-assault variables. Peer-group support for sexually aggressive behavior does appear to be relevant to the performance of this behavior, as do attitudes supportive of rape myths. Offenders also are more involved in all kinds of assaultive behavior generally than are the controls; however, the offenders are not characterized by more-traditional sex-roles attitudes or by more-liberal attitudes toward the use of violence.

Conclusions

In reflecting on the findings from the annual comparisons between offenders and controls, as well as the theoretical tests, several thoughts come to mind. First, all of the findings point to the fact that sexual-assault offenders are basically delinquent youth. Acceptance of this conclusion means that the comparisons between sexual-assault offenders and controls might be seen more appropriately as comparisons between delinquents and nondelinquents.[9] Sexually assaultive behavior is but one among many delinquent behaviors, all of which may be explained by the same set of variables. Thus, it is likely that the relationship between sexually assaultive behavior and any of the independent variables—Exposure to Delinquent Peers, for example—results from the joint connection of both of these factors to delinquent behavior generally.

Acknowledgment of this condition does not negate the previous findings, but it does limit them. While the findings show that sexual-assault offenders are basically delinquent youth and that they differ from nondelinquent youth in several specific ways, we do not know how they differ, if at all, from delinquent youth who have not committed any sexual assaults. To determine whether sexual-assault offenders may be distinguished from all other delinquents requires a comparison between two groups of delinquent youth, only one of which reports any sexual assaults.

These findings raise as many questions as they answer. Is sexually assaultive behavior influenced by variables other than those affecting involvement in delinquency generally? Are certain types of delinquency such as drug use and assaultive behavior more related to sexual assault than others? Under what conditions does sexually assaultive behavior occur outside a delinquent context and orientation? All of these issues and more remain for future research, but a thorough understanding of sexually assaultive behavior requires that they be addressed.

Second, we believe that the integrated delinquency model is the proper framework within which to study sexually assaultive behavior; however, our findings also have led to the conclusion that some revisions and adjustments are needed.

Despite the inconsistent results, we are inclined to believe that peer attitudes and behavior strongly influence sexually aggressive behavior. Prior research has noted consistently the importance of peer support for the performance of this behavior (Kanin 1967b; Polk et al. 1981). We believe that the two items employed as measures of peer support for sex and sexually aggressive behavior were relatively weak, indirect measures of this concept. They offered no direct information on the sexual aggressiveness of peers and only an indirect assessment of peer values regarding this behavior. More-relevant measures would inquire directly about both the behavior and the attitudes of peers regarding sexually aggressive behavior.

Further, the current items provide no indication of the importance the peer group places on this kind of behavior vis-à-vis other kinds of delinquent acts. How highly valued is sexual aggression within the continuum of acts that are rewarded and encouraged by the group? Logic and some prior research suggest that youth whose peer groups place a premium on this type of behavior will be more sexually aggressive.

In any future attempt to distinguish sexual-assault offenders from all other delinquents, a more-specialized set of sex-role and rape-myth scales may be important. Although their influence may not be direct, these attitudinal sets are associated with sexual aggression, as our own and prior research has shown (Polk et al. 1981; Abel, Blanchard, and Becker 1978; Abel, Madden, and Christopher 1975). While it has been argued that many male delinquents (criminals) hold depreciated images of women, it may be that those who engage in violence against women are the most extreme in this regard.

These considerations along with others may help to advance our thinking regarding adolescent sexual assault. From our perspective, theoretical progress in this area requires a full explication of the relationship between sexual assault and delinquent behavior generally. We are convinced that recurrent involvement in sexual assault is strongly related to a general delinquent life-style. Yet it is clear that not all delinquent youth commit sexual assaults. Identification of those factors that distinguish sexually assaultive delinquent youth from their delinquent counterparts who do not engage is such behavior is the next step in the advancement of theory in this area.

Notes

1. Rape myths are defined as prejudicial, stereotyped, or false beliefs about rape, rape victims, and offenders. Examples of rape myths include the following: "Most women secretly want to be raped," "Any healthy woman can resist a rapist," and "Rapists are sick, sexually deprived people."

2. The Normlessness t values and probability levels are as follows: Home Normlessness, $t = -3.23, p \leq .00$; School Normlessness, $t = -3.95, p \leq .00$; and Peer Normlessness, $t = -2.56, p \leq .01$.

3. The Negative Labeling t values and probability levels are as follows: Parental Negative Labeling, $t = -4.43, p \leq .00$; Teacher Negative Labeling, $t = -2.03, p \leq .05$; and Peer Negative Labeling, $t = -2.92, p \leq .01$.

4. Some of the variables that differentiate the groups were measured concurrently with the report of a sexual assault (in the same year period). Thus, for example, differences on the scale Exposure to Delinquent Peers reflect differences between the offenders and controls that occur simultaneously with the report of a sexual assault. Most of the distinguishing variables, however, reflect differences between the two groups after the sexual assault had occurred. A more-detailed discussion of these variables and the exact time period they cover occurs later in this chapter.

5. When the SAP began in 1978, we expanded the set of questions that could identify offenders. In 1976 and 1977, there was only one question about committing a sexual assault. Therefore it is possible that some of the offenders who reported in 1978 would have reported earlier if the broader set of questions had been in use.

6. We were unable to compare the groups on three of the theoretical scales since they were not available until 1978. The three scales are Attitudes toward Sex Roles, Attitudes toward Rape and Sexual Assault, and Attitudes toward Interpersonal Violence.

7. The combined peer involvement–exposure to delinquent peers measure is defined as the peer involvement (PI) score multiplied by the term exposure to delinquent peers (EDP) minus the mean of the exposure scale: $PI \times (EDP - \overline{EDP})$.

8. The problem of an excessive time lag (two years) is due to the causal ordering of the variables from the integrated delinquency model. For exam-

ple, conventional bonding variables such as Family and School Involvement predict bonding to delinquent peers, which predicts delinquent or sexually assaultive behavior. Using only interval estimates, there would be a two-year lag between the initial predictor variables (conventional bonding) and delinquency or sexual assault. We felt this was an unreasonable time lag and chose a shorter one by allowing the independent variables that were interval measures to be simultaneous with the report of a sexual assault.

9. Although we did not intend or design the control group to be nondelinquent, the fact that the majority of the NYS respondents reported little delinquency almost ensured this outcome.

**Part IV
An Overview of Adolescent
Sexual Assault**

10 Summary of Major Findings

A primary objective of the SAP research was to provide nationally representative estimates of the incidence and prevalence of sexual assault among adolescents. An assessment of the emotional and behavioral impact of a sexual assault on victims, both immediately and over some period of time, was also a central goal. An additional objective was the generation of basic descriptive data on victims, offenders, and the assault experience. Finally, the research was designed to test some ideas about vulnerability to sexual assault for adolescent females and the appropriateness of a delinquency model for explaining the commission of sexual assaults by male teenagers.

Prevalence and Incidence Estimates for Victims

In each year from 1978 to 1980, anywhere from 5 percent to 11 percent of the adolescent female population experienced at least one sexual assault. Taking into account the likelihood of a considerable amount of overreporting, a conservative estimate would be the low end of the .95 confidence interval, or around 5 to 7 percent. In actual numbers, these lower proportions indicate that from 700,000 to 1 million teenage females were sexually assaulted in each of the years analyzed. The rate of sexual assault was fairly constant across the three years.

The prevalence data show no significant race or social-class differences, although urban females are more vulnerable to sexual assault than are their rural peers. Although there is some variance by age in the prevalence of sexual assault, no consistent age trends emerge. These data on all sexual assaults do not support the popular notion that black lower-class females are more at risk than their white working-and middle-class peers.

The data indicate that from 1 million to 1.5 million sexual assaults occurred in each of the years analyzed (this is using the low end of the .95 confidence interval). The average frequency of sexual assault rose from 1978 to 1979 and then declined in 1980, so no clear trend may be discerned. No consistent significant differences in the incidence of sexual assault by race, age, social class, or place of residence were observed.

Overall a fairly constant proportion of adolescent females reported a sexual assault in each of the three years studied. The average frequency rose slightly but not substantially over the period. No dramatic increase in the prevalence or incidence of sexual assault among adolescent females was apparent. For both the prevalence and incidence data, no significant differences in the distribution of sexual assault by race, age, social class, or place of residence were observed, with one exception. The proportion of urban females reporting a sexual assault was significantly higher than that of the rural group, suggesting that population density does affect vulnerability to sexual assault.

The data also indicate that vulnerability to sexual assault increases sharply after an individual becomes a victim. Well over one-third of those who reported a sexual assault in 1978, 1979, and 1980 experienced at least one more sexual assault in the same year period. Over a two-year period, the data show that once having been sexually assaulted, the risk of another assault in the following year increases three to four times over the annual probability figure for all female adolescents. Clearly the risk of sexual assault rises dramatically once one has become a victim. Comparisons between victim and control groups suggest that involvement in delinquent behavior and with delinquent peers on the part of the victims may account for their initial and continuing vulnerability.

Comparisons of the Sexual Assault Project, National Crime Survey, and Uniform Crime Reports

To place the SAP findings in perspective, they were compared with data from the NCS and UCR, the only other national data on rape and sexual-assault victims. Comparisons across these three data sources indicate that the conclusions we draw about the incidence of rape and sexual assault will vary considerably depending on the data source consulted. Annually from 1978 through 1980, the UCR show a rate of substantially less than one report of forcible rape per 1,000 females. For this same time period, the NCS rate of forcible rape per 1,000 females is over ten times that of the UCR. The NCS are generally conceded to be much better estimates inasmuch as only a small portion of victims actually report to the police (the NCS data suggest only about half do).

Of more interest is the fact that the rate of serious, violent sexual assaults derived from the SAP is substantially higher than the rate of forcible rape drawn from the NCS. We suspect the NCS method of gathering data may dissuade adolescent females from reporting, and hence the NCS figures probably underestimate the actual amount of forcible rape for this popula-

Summary of Major Findings

tion. While both of these data sources are subject to underreporting and overreporting, we believe that the SAP procedures for gathering data are more likely to encourage the reporting of sexual assaults than are those of the NCS. Hence we believe the SAP annual rates to be the more-accurate estimates of physically violent assaults.

The sociodemographic profile of adolescent victims appears to vary most by the breadth or narrowness of one's definition of sexual assault. Victims of physically violent sexual assaults or forcible rapes appear to be typically black, lower-class, urban adolescents. In general both the NCS and SAP data sets confirm this image, though the data are not consistent on the racial part of this profile. When all sexual assaults are considered, not just those involving serious physical force, no race or social-class distinctions are noted, though urban females clearly are more at risk of a sexual assault.

The Sexual-Assault Experience from the Victim's View

All of the following descriptive data are based on the most-recent sexual assault among those reported annually by each victim. To the extent that most victims had only a single assault or that the most-recent event was typical of all the others, these descriptions may be generalized to all assaults.

For the majority of the victims, the assault occurred in one of three places: their home, the offender's home, or a vehicle. None of the victims reported that they had been hitchhiking prior to their victimization. With rare exception, the assaults involved one victim and one offender only.

According to the victims, the offenders were primarily boyfriends or dates. Less than 20 percent of the cases in each year involved unknown offenders, though the proportion of these cases more than doubled from 1978 to 1980. Given the social relationship between most of the victims and offenders, it is not surprising that most of the offenders were reported as being in the same age range as the victims.

The most-common force or pressure reported by the victims was verbal. Over half of the victims in each year reported this. From 27 percent to 40 percent mentioned some minimal physical force, while no more than 15 percent of the victims in any year reported a physical beating or the presence of a weapon. Nonetheless the proportion of victims reporting the more-serious types of physical force increased significantly from 1978 to 1980. These findings suggest that the greater mobility of older adolescent females, as well as their association with older males, increases the probability that they will confront more-serious physical pressure for sex.

The vast majority of the victims in each year offered verbal and/or physical resistance. In all three years, a majority of the victims were successful in deterring the assault, or other factors prevented the completion of the assault. The largest proportion of completed assaults occurred in 1980, when the victims reported experiencing the most physical force from the offenders.

Overall these data draw a picture of adolescent sexual assault as occurring primarily within the context of a date. It does not appear that the majority of these assaults involve serious physical force or conclude with physical injury to the victim. In fact, most probably would be classified as attempts. These data suggest that the greatest risk of sexual assault to teenage females is from a date or boyfriend, not a stranger encountered in a public place.

The Aftermath of Sexual Assault

One of the most-immediate decisions a victim must make is whether to inform the police of the sexual assault. Given the high number of attempted date rapes and the fact that sexual assaults are often not reported, it is not surprising that only 5 percent of the assaults from 1978 to 1980 were reported. Those that were tended to involve an unknown offender or multiple assailants. Furthermore, threats of violence and actual physical violence occurred in twice the proportion of reported as unreported assaults, and over half of the reported incidents were completed assaults as opposed to only 21 percent of the unreported ones. These findings lead to the conclusion that attempted nonviolent assaults by dates or boyfriends may not be defined by the victims as legitimate sexual assaults for purposes of reporting to officials.

With regard to the effect of an assault on personal relationships, the data indicate that over two-thirds of the victims tell their friends but not their parents. Friends were generally supportive and reassuring, as were those few parents who were informed. The data also suggest that personal relationships with husbands and boyfriends generally are not seriously affected by a sexual assault unless these individuals were the offenders. In these cases, the relationship has a high probability of ending.

In each of the three years analyzed, victims were asked to describe their reactions within a week of the assault. The strongest initial reactions in each year were anger, depression, and embarrassment. In addition, the large proportion (40 percent or more in each year) reporting some guilt reflects the ambivalence many sexual-assault victims feel about their role in the incident. The data also show that as the victims grew older and the assaults became more serious, the proportion of victims reporting negative reactions increased substantially. Aside from their initial reactions, the victims also described their feelings at the time of the interview, generally from one to six months after the assault. Without exception, the proportion of victims reporting each reaction had declined substantially. With the possible exception of anger and embarrassment, which are still reported by a sizable porportion of the victims, it would appear that the typical assault experience, a date rape, does not generate many negative reactions that persist even for six months.

Differential Response to a Sexual Assault

Initial reactions and those up to a year after the assault were analyzed by personal characteristics of the victim and various features of the assault experience. Reactions to the assault were not significantly differentiated by race, age at the time of the assault, social class, or place of residence. Among the assault variables, such as number of offenders, relationship to the offender, amount of force experienced, and whether the assault was completed, only the last had a significant influence on reactions. Victims who were able to deter the assault reported substantially fewer negative reactions within a year of the incident than did those who were assaulted. These findings seem to lead to several general conclusions. First, reactions to a sexual assault do not appear to be differentiated by demographic characteristics such as age or race. Second, the primary factor in the assault experience that appears to affect a victim's reactions is whether the assault was completed. And finally, since most of the assaults reported were of the same type, we believe there may not have been enough variability in the factors analyzed to produce many major differences in reactions. If, as the data suggest, multiple-offender and physically violent sexual assaults are relatively rare among adolescents, it may be exceedingly difficult ever to assess reliably the effect of these features on victim reactions, at least within a normal sample.

Long-Term Reactions to a Sexual Assault

For a portion of the victim sample, we were able to assess reactions to a sexual assault up to three years after its occurrence. For this group, reactions were assessed immediately after the assault and then at three later points: one to twelve months after the assault, thirteen to twenty-four months after, and twenty-five to thirty-six months after. The reactions reported within a week of the assault by the largest proportion were anger, embarrassment, depression, and guilt, just as for the full victim sample. At the first follow-up one to twelve months later, the proportion reporting each of the reactions declined substantially. This decline continued at the second follow-up for most reactions with a few notable exceptions. The proportion of victims reporting fear of being alone was substantially higher than what it had been initially, and the proportion reporting embarrassment and anger increased from the first follow-up.

By the final follow-up, some two to three years after the assault, the proportion of victims reporting several of the reactions had increased from the previous period, almost doubling in the case of depression. Regarding the reaction fear of being alone, the proportion at the final follow-up is the second highest reported, and the increase from the initial to the final measure is significant. These findings suggest that reactions may intensify with time and that relatively short follow-up periods of six months to a year after assault may not register some major effects because certain reactions have long incubation periods or are suppressed initially.

A case-by-case review of the victims with complete follow-up data showed that the pattern of reactions to an assault was not systematically ordered by any features of the assault experience or any of the social or demographic variables we analyzed. Victims with very comparable assault experiences in terms of the number of offenders, relationship to the offender, force experienced, and outcome reported very different reactions both initially and over time. It is possible that other factors not examined here, such as support from significant others, history of traumatic events, and personality traits, may be more instrumental in affecting long-term reactions to a sexual assault.

Vulnerability to Sexual Assault

Of primary interest in this research was the issue of differential risk. To explore this, we chose to focus on two factors believed associated with vulnerability: conventional sex-role socialization and attitudes, and untraditional, female role behavior and life-style. We compared the annual victim groups with randomly selected control groups on these two factors, as well as on a number of sociodemographic, sociopsychological, and environmental variables.

Demographically, the victims and controls were similar in all three years analyzed. The typical image of sexual-assault victims as black, lower-class, urban females was not supported by these data. We noted no significant differences between the groups on the Attitudes toward Sex Roles scale, suggesting that these attitudes are not especially relevant to sexual victimization.

The findings do indicate, however, that engaging in delinquent behavior and being part of a delinquent network influence the risk of being sexually assaulted. In all three years, the victims had significantly higher exposure to delinquent peers and were more involved in delinquent behavior than were the controls. It appears that teenage females who are generally delinquent are advertising their unconventionality in ways that jeopardize their control of sexual situations.

Additional analyses comparing the victims and controls prior to any reports of sexual victimization (in 1976 and 1977) indicate that the two groups were distinct even then. As much as two years prior to any reported sexual assaults, the victims and controls were substantially different in terms of peer networks, relations with family, and attitudes toward deviance. Although no significant differences in frequency of delinquency were observed in 1976 or 1977, a trend toward increasing involvement on the part of the victims was noted over this period.

The analyses clearly suggest that certain factors such as a delinquent peer group and involvement in delinquency may be predictive of sexual assault. When we used these and other relevant variables to attempt to classify the victim and control groups through a discriminant function analysis, however, we were able to classify correctly only 57 percent of the victims and 67 percent of the controls. While a delinquent life-style and peer network are related to the risk of sexual assault, they are only part of the picture. Accurate, reliable prediction of vulnerability to sexual assault requires the location of other factors influential in this process.

Prevalence and Incidence Estimates for Offenders

The prevalence and incidence results indicate that the proportion of male adolescents committing sexual assaults as well as the frequency with which these assaults occur declined from 1978 to 1980. Less than half as many males reported committing a sexual assault in 1980 as in 1978, and the incidence rate halved over this same period as well. This decline is not a simple function of maturation because the prevalence and incidence estimates for the same age groups across birth cohorts also declined. Finally, the demographic data indicate that the commission of sexual assault is fairly evenly distributed by race, social class, and place of residence.

In an attempt to place these findings in perspective, we compared them with data from the UCR and the NCS. Both of these sources gather data only on forcible rapes or attempts so the measure of forced sexual behavior is narrower than the one employed in the SAP. Only the incidence results could be compared since the UCR and NCS do not report prevalence data. Not surprisingly, the three data sets produce very different conclusions about the frequency of rape and sexual assault.

Based on victim reports, the NCS data indicate that adolescent males accounted for about 15 percent of the forcible rapes in 1978 and about 21 percent in 1979 (1980 data were not available). The rate of commission of forcible rape per 100,000 adolescent males jumped from 120 in 1978 to over 200 in 1979. By way of contrast, the UCR arrest data from 1978 through 1980 show an almost constant rate of arrest for forcible rape for males aged twelve to nineteen. There were approximately fifty arrests for forcible rape per year per 100,000 population of adolescent males.

Inasmuch as the SAP definition of sexual assault includes date rape, it is perhaps not surprising that the incidence figures are so much higher. Using the .95 confidence interval, the 1978 rate of sexual assault per 100,000 adolescent males ranges from 5,000 to 16,000. Assuming a considerable amount of underreporting, the upper bound of this .95 confidence interval is probably the more-accurate estimate. Although the incidence rate drops considerably by 1980, it is still substantially higher than either the NCS or UCR figures.

These disparate findings indicate that the conclusions we draw about the incidence of forced sexual behavior committed by adolescents will vary substantially by the unit of analysis (arrests or behavior) and the offense definition employed (forcible rape or sexual assault). The UCR are the most limited for estimations of incidence since they are based on arrests, which are more likely to reflect victim-reporting and police-processing practices than the actual occurrence of forcible rape. Although the NCS offer a far better estimate of the frequency of forcible rape, we believe this estimate is low due to underreporting by adolescent females. Finally, the SAP is the only source for national estimates of the incidence of all forced sexual behavior perpetrated by adolescent males.

Each of the three data sets examined measures a slightly different part of the rape and sexual-assault picture for adolescents. Individuals interested in the occurrence of forcible rape or arrests for such would do well to use the NCS and UCR, respectively. Those interested in the broader behavioral category of sexual assault would be better served by the SAP data. Careful attention to the unit of analysis (arrests or behavior) and the specific behavior of interest (forcible rape or sexual assault) should preclude the inappropriate use of any of these data sets.

Profiles of Adolescent Offenders

Both the SAP and UCR may be used to generate demographic profiles of adolescent offenders. The NCS are not as well suited for this purpose since offender profiles are derived from victim perceptions, which cannot include nonvisible traits such as social class. By comparing the offender profiles generated from the UCR and SAP, we may observe how youth arrested for forcible rape compare with all youth who commit sexual assaults.

Summary of Major Findings

For each year from 1978 through 1980, the UCR arrest data for forcible rape for youth eighteen years of age or younger present the following profile. Youth arrested for this crime are disproportionately black, urban adolescents. Although the UCR do not record the social class of those arrested, some research using selected police-arrest data has noted that rapists are typically from the lower socioeconomic group (Amir 1971; MacDonald 1971; Eisenhower 1969). Thus, police-arrest data describe the typical youthful rapist as a black, presumably lower-class adolescent residing in an urban area.

No such profile is evident in either the incidence or prevalence data from the SAP. From 1978 through 1980, no significant differences in the proportion of offenders or the frequency of offending were noted by race, social class, or place of residence.

The contrast between these two profiles is largely due to comparing arrests with behavior. The UCR profile of youthful rapists typifies only those who have been arrested, and they are only a subset of all youth who commit forcible rape. The SAP profile, on the other hand, is based on behavior, not arrests, and a larger category of forced sexual behavior than just forcible rape. For these reasons, we would expect sharp differences between the two profiles. The SAP profile should be a more-comprehensive and typical picture of adolescents who engage in sexually assaultive behavior.

The Sexual-Assault Experience from the Offender's View

These descriptions represent the most-recent sexual assault reported by each offender in each year from 1978 through 1980. To the extent that the most-recent assault for each offender is typical of all the others he committed in that year, the findings here are representative.

Most sexual assaults committed by adolescent males are spontaneous events that occur in the context of a date. The victims are typically girlfriends or dates of approximately the same age as the offender. Less than 15 percent of the victims in any one year were unknown to the offender. The offender's or victim's house was the typical setting for the assault.

Offenders view their own sexual excitement and the behavior and physical appearance of the victim as instrumental in causing the assault. A high proportion of the offenders had been drinking or taking drugs prior to the assault, and well over half of these reported that they were drunk or high when the assault occurred.

The primary type of force or pressure employed was verbal. Only a small proportion of offenders reported using much physical force. Few assaults involved weapons or more than one offender.

The offenders' reactions to the sexual assault reflect their own ambiguity about this experience. The feelings reported by the largest proportion of offenders include satisfied, confused, guilty, and proud. Reactions of friends who knew about the sexual assault were almost completely approving. Offenders appear to receive strong peer support from their friends for their sexually aggressive behavior.

Overall the picture of sexual assault provided by these adolescent offenders is one of date rape. Little in these data suggest that adolescent sexual assault typically or frequently involves serious physical violence or multiple offenders. A more-common situation would be a drunk or high teenage male attempting verbally to pressure or manipulate his date into having sex with him. Support for this sexually aggressive behavior appears to be strong among peers of the offender.

Prediction of Adolescent Sexual-Assault Offenders

Our explanation of sexually assaultive behavior is predicated on an integrated theory of delinquent behavior. We reasoned that sexual assault was but a type of delinquency and therefore ought to be predicted by generally the same set of variables. The delinquency model we employed is based on an integrated paradigm of social-control, strain, and social-learning theories. We revised the model slightly by adding several variables we felt would have particular relevance for sexual assault. These variables include Peer Support for Sexually Aggressive Behavior, Attitudes toward Sex Roles, Involvement in Assaultive Behavior, Attitudes toward Rape and Sexual Assault, and Attitudes toward Interpersonal Violence.

To assess the power of this model to predict sexually assaultive behavior, we conducted three sets of analyses. Initially we compared the offenders and a control group in 1978, 1979, and 1980 on a set of demographic and environmental variables, as well as all the theoretical variables. Next, in an attempt to ascertain whether any of the differences between the groups existed prior to the sexual-assault reports, we compared the offenders and controls on selected theoretical variables in 1976 and 1977. Finally, we ran a series of discriminant function analyses to see how well the set of theoretical variables could distinguish the offenders from the nonoffenders.

The initial static tests indicate that the two groups were basically similar demographically, with the exception that the offenders came from families that experienced significantly more crises such as divorce and extended unemployment. Other findings indicated that the offenders were substantially more estranged from their parents as well as being less attached to the school setting than were the controls.

Summary of Major Findings

The strongest findings from these analyses were associated with the peer group and involvement in delinquent behavior. For all three years, the sexual-assault offenders had significantly higher exposure to delinquent peers and received support from these friends for unconventional, delinquent acts, including sexual aggression. In addition, the offenders themselves were substantially more involved in delinquency, including serious offenses.

The findings did not support the notion that the offenders would hold more-traditional sex-role attitudes, be more accepting of rape myths, or be more willing to justify violent behavior. On all of these measures, the attitudinal set of the offenders was not significantly different from that of the controls.

The analyses on data gathered prior to any reported sexual assaults (in 1976 and 1977) reconfirmed many of the group differences observed after the assaults had been reported. Even before committing a sexual assault, the offender group could be distinguished from the controls in terms of their peer networks and generally greater involvement in delinquency. As much as two years prior to the first reported assaults, the offenders were less well integrated and committed to the home, family, and school than were the controls. These findings indicate that many of the differences preceded the sexual assaults and thus could logically be causal factors. To test this idea, a series of discriminant analyses were conducted to assess the combined effect of the variables to predict sexually assaultive behavior.

In the initial discriminant analysis, four variables contributed to the discrimination of the groups. In order of importance they were: Involvement with Delinquent Peers, Crimes against Persons, Attitudes toward Rape and Sexual Assault, and Family Normlessness. The combined power of these four variables correctly classified 77 percent of the cases, although approximately one-third of the offenders and 20 percent of the controls were incorrectly identified.

Inasmuch as so few of the added variables contributed to the discriminant function, we decided to test empirically our initial belief that the integrated delinquency model was not sufficient to account for sexually assaultive behavior. Consequently we conducted a second discriminant analysis using only the variables from the integrated delinquency model to see how well this model could distinguish the offenders and controls.

The only variable that contributed to the discrimination of the groups was Involvement with Delinquent Peers. By itself, it correctly classified 76 percent of the cases, with approximately the same error rate in offender and control-group assignment as for the full, revised model. Clearly the additional sexual-assault variables offer little improvement to the accuracy of the classification over that achieved with just one variable from the delinquency model. Since Involvement with Delinquent Peers entered first in both the discriminant analyses, it appears to be a primary factor in distinguishing offenders from nonoffenders.

In considering all the findings together, the results seem to reinforce the selection of the integrated delinquency model for explaining sexually assaultive behavior. Sexual-assault offenders appear to be youth who are not well integrated into the conventional social order, especially school, and are strongly bonded to delinquent peers. The offenders also report substantially more involvement in all types of delinquent behavior. It appears that these offenders fit a general delinquent profile in much the same way as youth who commit other offenses.

The data do not support the notion that youth who commit sexual assaults hold more-conventional sex-role attitudes or see physical violence as justifiable in more settings that do nonoffenders. Although it does appear that the variable, Attitudes toward Rape and Sexual Assault, contributes to the separation of the offenders from the controls, it is not critical to this process because its absence in the later analysis involving just delinquency variables had little effect on the accuracy of the classification. Overall these data seem to indicate that the explanation for sexual assault is not generally different from that for other types of illegal behavior committed by adolescents.

Acceptance of the conclusion that sexual-assault offenders are basically delinquent youth leads one to wonder whether the sexual-assault offender–control comparisons really represent just comparisons between delinquents and nondelinquents. If sexually assaultive behavior is explained by the same set of variables as delinquency in general, than the association between sexual assault and any of these variables may reflect simply their joint connection to delinquent behavior. This implies that the findings regarding sexual-assault offenders are not as definitive as we might have wished. To explicate the relationship between sexually assaultive behavior and delinquency in general, comparisons are needed between two groups of delinquent youth, only one of which reports any sexual assaults. Although we are convinced that recurrent involvement in sexual assault is related to a general delinquent life-style, our understanding of this relationship will be incomplete until we can distinguish delinquents who are sexually assaultive from those who are not.

11 Issues and Directions for Sexual-Assault Research

Rape and sexual-assault research generally suffers from a narrow focus on the behavior of interest. Treating rape and sexual assault as discrete, universally defined behavior belies the multidimensional character of forced sexual behavior and the public disagreement about what constitutes a rape or sexual assault. We believe along with Koss (1981) and Gibbons (1982) that sexually assaultive behavior is not unidimensional but comes in several forms and degrees. It should be conceptualized along a continuum of sexual behavior that ranges from conventional sexual behavior (consensual, nonassaultive sexual acts) to that involving violent, physical force. By studying the range of sexually aggressive behavior that occurs, we may discover the frequency of all types of sexual aggression, as well as locate the point (or points) where this behavior moves from socially acceptable to unacceptable to criminal behavior.

Most research in this area, our own included, has not conceptualized or operationalized sexual assault on a comprehensive continuum. The one exception that we know of is the work of Koss (1981). More efforts that collect data on the full range of sexually assaultive behavior are necessary if we are to understand the varieties of this behavior, the incidence and prevalence of the different types, differential victim response by type of assault, and the characteristics of offenders associated with the various kinds of sexually aggressive behavior.

The limited definitional approach to rape and sexual assault grew out of clinical work with victims and the use of police data that focus on forcible rape. Our conceptualization of this behavior must become more sophisticated. Continued attention to specific forms of sexual assault to the exclusion of the full range will hinder the advancement of our knowledge and understanding of this multidimensional phenomenon.

There are at least two important factors to consider in the development of a continuum of sexually assaultive behavior.

First, questions about the different types or degrees of sexual assault must contain as precise behavioral descriptions of the forced sexual behavior as possible and reasonable. Questions that ask about being sexually assaulted or raped by using these words independent of behavioral definitions may elicit no or few responses because of ambiguity and disagreement about the meaning of these words. The fact that victims do not always define physically coerced sex as rape or sexual assault has been documented (Koss 1981; Zellman et al. 1981).

Second, the initial questions should be followed by an attempt to elicit a full description of the event, including all of the sexual acts involved. It is not possible to capture in the opening questions all combinations of such acts, yet knowledge of the constellation of sexually assaultive behavior experienced is critical to assessing outcome for victims as well as differentiating types of offenders. We are painfully aware of these issues because our own research, by virtue of being a secondary study, was restricted from gathering full descriptions of the sexual behavior that occurred.

Given the essentially interactive nature of sexual assault, it is ironic that most rape research has been conducted on victims and offenders as separate groups. The basic unit in a sexual assault is the victim-offender dyad, yet to our knowledge no behavioral studies of this unit exist. This is so despite the fact that the rape situation, especially the date rape, has been conceptualized as a consequence of the misreading or miscommunicating of sexual cues and scripts.

While the basic difficulties (especially human subject concerns) involved in studying actual dyads of rape victims and offenders are obvious, there are other methods by which to study the human dynamics surrounding rape and sexual assault. What is important is that we begin to describe the sequence of behaviors, gestures, cues, and circumstances that constitute a sexually assaultive incident. Following this descriptive process should be an explanatory one in which we look for patterns or sequences of interaction that lead to particular outcomes, such as an attempted or completed rape or the presence or absence of physical injury to the victim. Understanding the victim-offender dynamics that precede and continue during a sexual assault is central to developing an explanation for the occurrence of sexual assault, as well as developing effective prevention and resistance advice for victims.

A final concern is directed to the general lack of theoretical and methodological sophistication in rape and sexual-assault research. As is the case with most emerging fields of inquiry, the initial rape studies were often descriptive and based on small, purposive samples. This early work provided needed information where none or little existed and helped to generate an interest in this area of research, but now we are at a stage where advancement of knowledge requires theoretically grounded, methodologically rigorous research efforts. Concerns about the reliability and validity of sexual-assault data, the appropriateness of samples for the research questions being asked, and the applicability of findings to larger populations need to be addressed. We need to be increasingly concerned about the accuracy of data based on long recall periods, the general absence of control groups from much rape research, the biases introduced when using known group samples, and limitations imposed by the manner in which questions are posed. All of these issues and others require attention if rape research is to progress.

From a theoretical perspective, we perceive a need for two primary efforts operating stimultaneously. The first is to review and integrate the myriad of results we have generated regarding the causes and consequences of sexually assaultive behavior. Those findings that are conceptually sound and have some empirical support should be subjected to systematic, methodologically rigorous testing in order to consolidate existing knowledge. Parallel to this effort should be an endeavor to fill in the theoretical voids, to develop explanations for those parts of the sexual-assault puzzle not yet addressed. Ideally these two efforts should mesh so that new theorizing is guided by prior knowledge.

We have tried to raise some general concerns we believe are critical to the advancement of rape and sexual-assault research. We are not unique in raising these issues, for others have expressed the same or similar concerns about the state of work in this area. We add our voices to the others in the hope of drawing attention to gaps and weaknesses in the existing research and encouraging others to address those issues that have been relatively untended in this field. Sexual-assault research is no longer in its infancy, but it has not yet come of age either.

Appendix A: Description of Attitudinal and Behavioral Scales

Attitudinal and Behavioral Scales

A five-point response set ranging from "Strongly Agree" to "Strongly Disagree" was employed with the following scales.

Attitudes toward Sex Roles: A nine-item scale designed to measure attitudes about the appropriate behavior and roles for men and women. A high score indicates traditional or conventional sex-role attitudes. Sample item: "It is the women's job to take care of the home and the children."

Attitudes toward Interpersonal Violence: A nine-item scale designed to measure attitudes about the acceptability of violence under various circumstances. A high score signifies acceptance of violence as a means to handle a variety of interpersonal situations. Sample item: "It is alright to physically beat up people who call you names."

Attitudes toward Rape and Sexual Assault: A seven-item scale designed to measure beliefs about rape and sexual assault. A high score indicates adherence to traditional rape myths. Sample item: "Any healthy woman can resist a rapist."

Perceived Negative Labeling: A set of four twelve-item scales that measure perceptions of negative labeling by parents, friends, teachers, and coworkers. A high score refects negative labeling. Sample item: "How much would your [parents, friends, teachers, or coworkers] agree that you have a lot of personal problems?"

Social Isolation: A set of three five-item scales designed to assess estrangement from three separate social contexts: home, school, and the peer group. A high score indicates alienation from each context. Sample item: "I feel like an outsider with my [family, friends] or at school."

Normlessness: A set of three four-item scales designed to measure the belief that one has to break rules to achieve conventional goals at school, at home, and with peers. A high score reflects a high commitment to the conventional norms in each context. Sample item: "Making a good impression is more important than telling the truth to [friends, parents, or teachers]."

A four-point response set ranging from "Very Wrong" to "Not Wrong at All" was used with this scale.

Attitudes toward Deviance: A nine-item scale designed to assess personal beliefs regarding the wrongness of certain types of delinquent behavior. A high score reflects a conventional prosocial orientation toward behavior. Sample item: "How wrong is it for someone your age to get drunk once in a while?"

A five-point response set ranging from "All of Them" to "None of Them" was used with this scale.

Exposure to Delinquent Peers: A thirteen-item scale designed to measure the involvement of peers in delinquent behavior. A high score indicates high exposure to delinquent peers. Sample item: "During the last year how many of your friends have broken into a vehicle or building to steal something?"

A five-point response set ranging from "Strongly Disapprove" to "Strongly Approve" was used with these two scales.

Perceived Peer and Parental Disapproval of Delinquent Behavior: Two separate eleven-item scales designed to assess the nature of the peer and parental sanctioning networks regarding delinquent behavior. A high score signifies conventional disapproval of delinquent behavior. Sample item: "How would your [parents or friends] react if you stole something worth more than $50?"

A three-point response set composed of "Yes," "Don't Know," and "No" was used with this measure.

Commitment to Delinquent Peers: A three-item measure that assesses support for delinquent or antisocial peers. A high score indicates support for these friends. Sample item: "If your friends got into trouble with the police, would you be willing to lie to protect them?"

Two response sets are used with the involvement measures. The first, a response set from 0 to 5 reflects the number of afternoons and evenings in an average week spent on each activity. The second uses a five-point scale ranging from "A Great Deal" to "Very Little" to report time spent on the weekend.

Family, School, and Peer Involvement Measures: These three measures reflect the amount of time spent with the family, with peers, and on academic concerns. A high score indicates a high level of involvement with family, peers or academic matters. Sample item: "On the average, how many weekday evenings, Monday through Friday, from dinnertime to bedtime, have you spent on [family activities, with friends, or studying]?"

Two three-point response sets are used with these scales. The first measures aspirations and includes "Very Important," "Somewhat Important" and "Not Important at All." The second measures achievement relative to aspiration and includes "Very Well," "O.K.," and "Not Well at All."

Aspirations and Achievement: Two five-item scales that reflect aspirations and perceived achievement at home and school. A high score indicates high aspirations and/or achievement of those aspirations. Sample item: "How important is it to you to get along well with your parents [at school]? How well are you doing at this?"

A four-point response set ranging from "Never" to "Often" is used with this scale.

Peer Pressure for Drinking and Drug Use: A six-item scale reflecting pressure from friends for alcohol and drug use. A high score signifies high pressure. Sample item: "During the last year, how often have your friends put pressure on you to drink?"

A five-point response set ranging from "Never" to "More than Six Times" is used with the following two scales.

Trouble from Drinking: A scale designed to measure problems associated with use of alcohol. A high score indicates problems from drinking. Sample item: "How many times in the last year have you had problems with your family because of drinking?"

Trouble from Drug Use: The intent and scoring of the scale is the same as for the scale Trouble from Drinking.

Family Crises: A measure reflecting the number of disruptive events such as divorce and long-term unemployment that have occurred in the respondent's home in the past year. The score indicates the actual number of family crises reported.

Three single-item measures were used in the SAP research. The first, Attendance at Religious Services, reflects church participation on a five-point scale ranging from "Never" to "Several Times a Week." A high score indicates more participation.

The second and third items measure Peer Disapproval of Sexual Intercourse and Forced Sex. These items are measured on a five-point scale ranging from "Strongly Disapprove" to "Strongly Approve." A high score signifies lack of approval for each behavior, respectively.

Delinquency and Victimization Scales

An open-ended frequency count was used as a response set for all the delinquency and victimization scales. Thus, the higher the score, the higher the reported delinquency or victimization..

Felony Assault: Aggravated assault; Sexual assault; Gang fights.

Minor Assault: Hit teacher; Hit parent; Hit student.

Robbery: Strong-armed students; Strong-armed teachers; Strong-armed others.

Felony Theft: Stole motor vehicle; Stole something greater than $50; Broke into building/vehicle; Bought stolen goods.

Minor Theft: Stole something less than $5; Stole something $5/50; Joyriding.

Damaged Property: Damaged family property; Damaged school property; Damaged other property.

Illicit Drug Use: Hallucinogens; Heroin; Amphetamines; Cocaine; Barbiturates.

Deviant Life-Style: Runaway; Sexual intercourse; Public drunkenness; Hitchhiked; Prostitution.

Illegal Services: Prostitution; Sold marijuana; Sold hard drugs.

Public Disorder: Hitchhiked; Panhandled; Disorderly conduct; Obscene calls; Public drunkenness.

Status Offenses: Runaway; Skipped classes; Lied about age; Sexual intercourse.

Appendix A

Crimes against Persons: Aggravated assault; Sexual assault; Gang fights; Strong-armed students; Strong-armed teachers; Strong-armed others; Hit teacher; Hit parent; Hit student.

General Theft: Stole motor vehicle; Stole something less than $5; Stole something $5/50; Stole something greater than $50; Broke into building/vehicle; Bought stolen goods; Joyriding.

School Delinquency: Damaged school property; Strong-armed students; Strong-armed teachers; Cheated on school test; Hit teacher; Hit student; Stole at school; Skipped classes.

Home Delinquency: Damaged family property; Runaway; Stolen from family; Hit parent.

Index Offenses: Aggravated assault; Sexual assault; Gang fights; Stole motor vehicle; Stole something greater than $50; Broke into building/vehicle; Strong-armed students; Strong-armed teachers; Strong-armed others.

Non-sexual Victimization: Beaten by parents; Beaten by someone other than parents; Attacked with a weapon; Car, motorcycle, or bicycle stolen; Things stolen from car, bike, or motorcycle; Personal property damaged; Personal property stolen from a public place; Pocket picked, purse or wallet snatched.

General Delinquency A: Damaged family property; Damaged school property; Damaged other property; Stole motor vehicle; Stole something greater than $50; Bought stolen goods; Runaway; Lied about age; Carried hidden weapon; Stole something less than $5; Aggravated assault; Prostitution; Sexual intercourse; Gang fights; Sold marijuana; Hitchhiked; Hit teacher; Hit parent; Hit student; Disorderly conduct; Sold hard drugs; Joyriding; Liquor for minor; Sexual assault; Strong-armed students; Strong-armed teachers; Strong-armed others; Evaded payment; Public drunkenness; Stole something $5/50; Broke into building/vehicle; Panhandled; Skipped classes; Didn't return change; Obscene calls.

General Delinquency B: Stole motor vehicle; Stole something greater than $50; Bought stolen goods; Runaway; Carried hidden weapon; Stole something less than $5; Aggravated assault; Prostitution; Sexual intercourse; Gang fights; Sold marijuana; Hit teacher; Hit parent; Hit student; Disorderly conduct; Sold hard drugs; Joyriding; Sexual assault; Strong-armed students; Strong-armed teachers; Strong-armed others; Stole something $5/50; Broke into building/vehicle; Panhandled.

Appendix B: Scale Reliabilities

Table B-1
Scale Reliabilities and Homogeneity Ratios

Scale Name	Cronbach's Coefficient Alpha[a]	Scott's Homogeneity Ratio[b]
Attitudes toward Sex Roles	.80	.31
Attitudes toward Interpersonal Violence	.80	.33
Attitudes toward Rape and Sexual Assault	.75	.25
Perceived Negative Labeling		
Family	.86	.34
Peers	.85	.34
Teachers	.89	.41
Social Isolation		
Family	.79	.44
Peers	.74	.37
School	.66	.28
Normlessness		
Family	.69	.37
Peers	.63	.31
School	.68	.30
Attitudes toward Deviance	.84	.40
Exposure to Delinquent Peers	.83	.37
Perceived Disapproval of Delinquent Behavior		
Parents	.84	.38
Peers	.89	.49
Involvement		
Family	.73	.50
Peers	.68	.42
School	.66	.42
Aspirations		
Family	.76	.40
Peer	.65	.32
Academic	.78	.41
Achievement Relative to Aspirations		
Family	.79	.43
Peer	.66	.33
Academic	.76	.39
Peer Pressure for Drinking/Drug Use[c]	.75	.38
Trouble from Drinking[c]	.69	.32
Trouble from Drug Use[c]	.65	.30

Note: All of these reliabilities and homogeneity ratios are from the third survey, 1978. Since the values across the five years were quite similar, we used the middle year to represent the reliabilities and homogeneity ratios.

[a]Cronbach's Coefficient Alpha (Cronbach 1951) estimates the reliability of a scale by examining its internal consistency. A measure of internal consistency, such as Cronbach's Alpha, assumes that each of the items in a scale measures a single trait or attribute and that all items do so equally well. Under this assumption, any random subset of items from a scale

Reliability Testing of Self-Report Delinquency Scales

Inasmuch as self-report delinquency scales are not unidimensional or homogeneous, the use of internal consistency measures of reliability such as Cronbach's Coefficient Alpha is inappropriate. Hence, a test-retest estimate of reliability was used.

A sample of the 1980 NYS respondents stratified by race and level of delinquency involvement was selected to be reinterviewed. All respondents in the retest sample were contacted during the fourth week following their original interview. Every effort was made to complete the retest interview with the same interviewer and in the same location as originally.

Three measures of the reliability of various NYS self-reported delinquency scales are presented in table B-2. The product-moment correlation between test and retest scores is provided for two different scoring schemes. The first scoring scheme reflects the sum of the frequency responses to the items comprising each scale. The second is a variety score, which counts the number of different delinquent behaviors in each scale that respondents indicated they had committed during the past year. The final estimate of reliability or response consistency is the percentage of each sample whose difference between test and retest scores on the frequency scored scales is two or less. This is a rather stringent test, especially for scales involving high-frequency items.

Table B-2 indicates that the vast majority of the test-retest correlations for both frequency-scored and variety-scored scales are in the .60 to .90 range. The correlation scores suggest, however, that the reliability of the Minor Assault Scale is considerably less than that of the other scales. Also, it is clear that the reliabilities of some scales shift dramatically depending on whether a frequency or a variety score is used in the correlations.

Examination of the percentages of respondents who reported essentially he same frequency score on both the test and retest indicates a high level of consistency in responses across most of the scales. Inasmuch as the

---

is equivalent to any other random subset of the same number, and an estimate of reliability is the average intercorrelation of all of the potential random subsets. The value of Cronbach's Coefficient Alpha typically ranges from 0.00 to 1.00. While there are differences of opinion as to what constitutes an acceptable level of reliability, alphas of .60 or higher are generally accepted.

[b]Scott's Homogeneity Ratio (Scott 1968) reflects the weighted average interitem correlation of a scale. It represents a check on the additive assumption involved in scaling and provides an indication of the overlap of all items in a scale. Homogeneity ratios typically range from 0.00 to 1.00, with the former value indicating no correlation among the items and the latter reflecting perfect correlation. It has been suggested that .33 is an optimum value, reflecting moderate interitem correlation without too much redundancy. In practice, a homogeneity ratio between .20 and .50 is considered satisfactory.

[c]The reliability and homogeneity ratio scores for these scales are from 1979 since these scales were not available for all subjects in 1978.

Appendix B

General Delinquency B score is a summation of most of the items and thus is susceptible to error in all items, it is not surprising that it reflects the lowest test-retest agreement. The Public Disorder and Status Offense scales also are lower in test-retest consistency, but both have several items of high frequency, such as sexual intercourse and disorderly conduct.

In sum, the reliability as indicated by either absolute accuracy or by the test-retest correlations (or both) appears adequate for all of the scales with the exception of Minor Assault and Status Offenses. There is also an indication from some of the group-specific analyses not presented here that the Property Damage scale may not be as reliable as the others (Huizinga and Elliott 1982). Although the General Delinquency B scale had a low test-retest consistency, the correlations are consistently high, indicating an acceptable reliability.

A thorough technical discussion of the reliability of these scales, including a description of the reliabilities for demographic subgroups, may be found in Huizinga and Elliott (1982).

Table B-2
Reliability Indexes for Various Self-Report Delinquency Scales: Retest Sample (N = 177)

Delinquency Scales	Correlation Frequency Scores	Correlation Variety Scores	Percent of Sample with Test-Retest Difference of 2 or less
General Delinquency B	.750	.844	37.8
Index Offenses	.651	.869	97.0
Felony Assault	.673	.762	98.3
Minor Assault	.585	.565	84.6
Robbery	.837	.747	99.4
Felony Theft	.523	.884	98.9
Minor Theft	.802	.759	96.6
Property Damage	.880	.578	91.5
Illegal Services	.930	.792	93.8
Public Disorder	.915	.691	66.9
Status Offenses	.489	.798	50.0

Appendix C: Sexual-Assault Questions

SEXUAL ASSAULT OFFENDER QUESTIONS

The following set of questions are related to the event you reported earlier in the interview of having pressured someone to do more sexually than they wanted to do. For purposes of this interview, we are interested in the sexual situation in which contact with the private parts of your body or another person's body was brought about by pressure from you. Please remember that all your answers are confidential and that your name will not appear anywhere on the interview.

(AT THIS POINT, IT IS POSSIBLE THE RESPONDENT WILL SAY THAT WHAT HE/SHE REPORTED DOES NOT FALL WITHIN OUR DEFINITION AS STATED ABOVE. IF THE RESPONDENT DOES NOT VOLUNTARILY DESCRIBE WHAT HE/SHE DID DO, GO BACK TO THE BLOCKED ITEM AND ASK, "What did you mean when you said that (READ BLOCKED ITEM)?" RECORD RESPONSE BUT DO NOT PROBE FURTHER IF RESPONDENT IS EMBARRASSED, HOSTILE, ETC. IF YOU SUSPECT THE RESPONDENT HAS CHANGED HIS/HER ANSWER TO AVOID THE OFFENDER QUESTIONS, PLEASE INDICATE WHAT MADE YOU THINK THIS.)_____

_____

_____

(IF RESPONDENT REFUSES OFFENDER QUESTIONS, SKIP TO QUESTION 400, PAGE 74.)_____

Before beginning, remember that we are talking about the *most recent event*.

382. When did the event take place? (DO NOT READ THE FOLLOWING LIST.)

   ____ (1) January - March, 1980[a]
   ____ (2) April - June, 1980
   ____ (3) July - September, 1980
   ____ (4) October - December, 1980

Note: The parts of the interview in parentheses and capital letters are interviewer instructions.

a These are the appropriate dates for the final interview. This item was focused on 1978 and 1979 respectively in the first two interviews.

383. Where did the event take place? (DO NOT READ THE FOLLOWING LIST. CHECK ALL THAT APPLY. DO NOT ALLOW PLACE NAMES SUCH AS CHICAGO, NEW YORK, ETC.)

   ____ (1) Victim's house or apartment
   ____ (2) Offender's house or apartment
   ____ (3) Someone else's house or apartment
   ____ (4) Other buildings or enclosed structures (such as schools, stairwells, empty buildings, etc.)
   ____ (5) Motel/hotel room
   ____ (6) Car, van, truck or other vehicle
   ____ (7) Street or alley
   ____ (8) Other outside (such as beach, field, in the hills or mountains, backyard, etc.)
   ____ (9) Other (SPECIFY) _____

384. How many people did you pressure or force?
   ____ (1) One
   ____ (2) Two
   ____ (3) Three
   ____ (4) More than three

385. What was the sex of the person(s)? (THIS ITEM REFERS TO THE SEX OF THE VICTIM(S).)
   ____ (1) Male
   ____ (2) Female
   ____ (3) Both

386. Did you know the person(s)? (IF MULTIPLE VICTIMS AND SOME ARE KNOWN AND SOME ARE NOT, CIRCLE BOTH YES AND NO AND ASK QUESTION 387 FOR THE KNOWN VICTIM(S).)

            Yes   No   (IF NO, SKIP TO QUESTION 388, PAGE 72)
             2   1

387. Was the person(s) your . . . (READ THE LIST. IF MORE THAN ONE VICTIM, CHECK ALL THAT APPLY. IF MORE THAN ONE CATEGORY APPLIES TO A SINGLE VICTIM, CHECK ALL THAT APPLY.)

   IF MALE VICTIM   IF FEMALE VICTIM

   ____ (1) Boyfriend   ____ (1) Girlfriend
   ____ (2) Date   ____ (2) Date
   ____ (3) Friend   ____ (3) Friend
   ____ (4) Acquaintance   ____ (4) Acquaintance
   ____ (5) Brother   ____ (5) Sister
   ____ (6) Father   ____ (6) Mother
   ____ (7) Husband   ____ (7) Wife
   ____ (8) Other (SPECIFY)   ____ (8) Other (SPECIFY)
        _____   _____

Appendix C   155

388. Approximately how old was the person(s)? (DO NOT READ THE FOLLOWING LIST. IF MORE THAN ONE VICTIM, CHECK ALL THAT APPLY.)

         ____ (1) 10 and under   ____ (5) 25 - 34
         ____ (2) 11 - 15   ____ (6) 35 - 49
         ____ (3) 16 - 19   ____ (7) 50 - 64
         ____ (4) 20 - 24   ____ (8) 65 and older

389. Was the person(s) hitchhiking?
              Yes   No
               2   1

390. Which of the following kinds of pressure or force, if any, did you use? (READ THE LIST AND CIRCLE THE APPROPRIATE RESPONSES.)

     YES   NO

      2   1   (1) Verbal persuasion, such as "If you love me, you will" or "I'll break up with you if you don't"
      2   1   (2) Verbal threats to tell others of the event or something embarrassing or bad about the person
      2   1   (3) Verbal threats of injury
      2   1   (4) Taking the person(s) by surprise
      2   1   (5) Drugging the person(s) or getting them drunk
      2   1   (6) Pushing, slapping and mild roughness
      2   1   (7) Display of a weapon such as a knife, bottle or cigarette lighter
      2   1   (8) Physical beating and/or choking
      2   1   (9) Injury from a weapon such as cutting with a knife or burning with a lighter
      2   1   (10) The person(s) was afraid of your size and strength
      2   1   (11) There were others with you
                        IF YES: "How many others not counting yourself?" ____
                        (THIS COUNT SHOULD NOT INCLUDE THE VICTIM(S).)
      2   1   (12) Other (SPECIFY) _____

391. Were you successful in your attempt?

              No   Yes   (IF YES, SKIP TO QUESTION 393, PAGE 73)
               1   2

392. Why not? (DO NOT READ THE LIST. CHECK ALL THAT APPLY.)

         ____ (1) Victim resistance or rejection
         ____ (2) Offender scared, guilty or concerned
         ____ (3) Offender lost interest, didn't pursue act
         ____ (4) Act interrupted
         ____ (5) Other (SPECIFY) _____

393. From the three statements I am going to read you, select the one which best describes the event. (READ EACH STATEMENT AND CIRCLE THE APPROPRIATE RESPONSES. ONLY ONE YES SHOULD BE CIRCLED.)

YES	NO		
2	1	(1)	The event was arranged beforehand, you thought about it and planned things to make it happen.
2	1	(2)	The event was not arranged beforehand, but you had thought about it before it happened.
2	1	(3)	The event was neither arranged nor thought about beforehand, it just happened.

(IF YES TO (1), ASK:) How did you plan it? _____

394. In your opinion, how much did the following things contribute, if at all, to the event happening? Choose your answers from Card number 11, the second white card. (READ THE FOLLOWING LIST AND RECORD A RESPONSE FOR EACH ITEM.)

How much did each contribute to the event happening?	Not at All	Very Little	Some	Quite A Bit	A Great Deal	(DON'T KNOW)
The location such as a dark street or place without many people around	1	2	3	4	5	____
The time of day	1	2	3	4	5	____
The type of activity in which you were involved such as partying, being out with your friends, etc.	1	2	3	4	5	____
Your being drunk or high	1	2	3	4	5	____
Your being a violent person	1	2	3	4	5	____
Your being sexually excited	1	2	3	4	5	____
Your having emotional problems	1	2	3	4	5	____
The person(s) being drunk or high	1	2	3	4	5	____
The person(s) clothes, jewelry or make-up	1	2	3	4	5	____
The person(s) physical build	1	2	3	4	5	____
The person(s) flirting or teasing	1	2	3	4	5	____

Appendix C

	Not at All	Very Little	Some	Quite A Bit	A Great Deal	(DON'T KNOW)
The person(s) being sexually excited	1	2	3	4	5	____
The type of activity in which the person(s) was involved such as partying, hitchhiking, etc.	1	2	3	4	5	____
Other (SPECIFY)_____	1	2	3	4	5	____

395. Had you been drinking or taking drugs before the event?

    Yes No
     2   1   (IF NO, SKIP TO QUESTION 397)

396. Would you say you were drunk or high during the event?

    Yes No
     2   1

397. Do any of your close friends know about the event?

    Yes No
     2   1   (IF NO, SKIP TO QUESTION 399)

398. Which of the following statements, if any, describe their reactions? Did they . . .
(READ THE LIST AND CIRCLE THE APPROPRIATE RESPONSES.)

YES	NO		
2	1	(1)	Approve of what you did
2	1	(2)	Disapprove of what you did
2	1	(3)	Other (SPECIFY) _____
2	1	(4)	Didn't react one way or the other

399. Which of the following statements, if any, describe your reactions after the event? (READ THE LIST AND CIRCLE THE APPROPRIATE RESPONSES.)

YES	NO		
2	1	(1)	Proud
2	1	(2)	Embarrassed
2	1	(3)	Satisfied
2	1	(4)	Powerful
2	1	(5)	Guilty
2	1	(6)	Confused, sort of good and sort of bad
2	1	(7)	Other (SPECIFY) _____

(PLEASE THANK THE RESPONDENT BY SAYING:) We want you to know that we appreciate your willingness to share a personal experience with us.

SEXUAL ASSAULT VICTIM QUESTIONS

The following set of questions are related to the event you reported earlier in the interview of having been pressured by someone to do more sexually than you wanted to do. For purposes of this interview, we are interested in the sexual situation in which someone pressured you into contact with the private parts of your body or theirs. Please remember that all your answers are confidential and that your name will not appear anywhere on the interview.

(AT THIS POINT, IT IS POSSIBLE THE RESPONDENT WILL SAY THAT WHAT HE/SHE REPORTED DOES NOT FALL WITHIN OUR DEFINITION AS STATED ABOVE. IF THE RESPONDENT DOES NOT VOLUNTARILY DESCRIBE WHAT HAPPENED, GO BACK TO THE BLOCKED ITEM AND ASK, "What did you mean when you said that (READ BLOCKED ITEM)?" RECORD RESPONSE BUT DO NOT PROBE FURTHER IF RESPONDENT IS EMBARRASSED, HOSTILE, ETC. IF YOU SUSPECT THE RESPONDENT HAS CHANGED HIS/HER ANSWER TO AVOID THE VICTIM QUESTIONS, PLEASE INDICATE WHAT MADE YOU THINK THIS.)

_____
_____
_____

(IF RESPONDENT REFUSES VICTIM QUESTIONS, SKIP TO QUESTION 433, PAGE 86.)_____)

Before beginning, remember that we are talking about the <u>most recent event.</u>

401. When did the event take place? (DO NOT READ THE FOLLOWING LIST.)

    ____ (1) January - March, 1980
    ____ (2) April - June, 1980
    ____ (3) July - September, 1980
    ____ (4) October - December, 1980

402. Where did the event take place? (DO NOT READ THE FOLLOWING LIST. CHECK ALL THAT APPLY. DO NOT ALLOW PLACE NAMES SUCH AS CHICAGO, NEW YORK, ETC.)

    ____ (1) Victim's house or apartment
    ____ (2) Offender's house or apartment
    ____ (3) Someone else's house or apartment
    ____ (4) Other buildings or enclosed structures (such as schools, stairwells, empty buildings, etc.)
    ____ (5) Motel/hotel room
    ____ (6) Car, van, truck or other vehicle
    ____ (7) Street or alley
    ____ (8) Other outside (such as beach, field, in the hills or mountains, backyard, etc.)
    ____ (9) Other (SPECIFY) _____

403. Did the event take place in your neighborhood or the area in which you lived for most of last year?

    Yes   No
    2   1

404. Were you hitchhiking when the event occurred?

    Yes   No
    2   1

Appendix C

405. Were you the only one who was pressured or forced?

    No   Yes   (IF YES, SKIP TO QUESTION 407)
    1   2

406. How many others were there?

    ____ (1) One
    ____ (2) Two
    ____ (3) Three
    ____ (4) More than three

407. How many people were involved in pressuring or forcing you?

    ____ (1) One
    ____ (2) Two
    ____ (3) Three
    ____ (4) More than three

408. What was the sex of the person(s) involved? (THIS ITEM REFERS TO THE SEX OF THE OFFENDER(S).)

    ____ (1) Male
    ____ (2) Female
    ____ (3) Both

409. Did you know the person(s)? (IF MULTIPLE OFFENDERS AND SOME ARE KNOWN AND SOME ARE NOT, CIRCLE BOTH YES AND NO AND ASK QUESTION 410 FOR THE KNOWN OFFENDER(S).)

    Yes   No   (IF NO, SKIP TO QUESTION 411, PAGE 77)
    2   1

410. Was the person(s) your . . . (READ THE LIST. IF MORE THAN ONE OFFENDER, CHECK ALL THAT APPLY. IF MORE THAN ONE CATEGORY APPLIES TO A SINGLE OFFENDER, CHECK ALL THAT APPLY.)

IF MALE OFFENDER	IF FEMALE OFFENDER
____ (1) Boyfriend	____ (1) Girlfriend
____ (2) Date	____ (2) Date
____ (3) Friend	____ (3) Friend
____ (4) Acquaintance	____ (4) Acquaintance
____ (5) Brother	____ (5) Sister
____ (6) Father	____ (6) Mother
____ (7) Husband	____ (7) Wife
____ (8) Other (SPECIFY) _____	____ (8) Other (SPECIFY) _____

411. Approximately how old was the person(s)? (DO NOT READ THE FOLLOWING LIST. IF MORE THAN ONE OFFENDER, CHECK ALL THAT APPLY.)

    ____ (1) 10 and under   ____ (5) 25 - 34
    ____ (2) 11 - 15   ____ (6) 35 - 49
    ____ (3) 16 - 19   ____ (7) 50 - 64
    ____ (4) 20 - 24   ____ (8) 65 and older

412. Which of the following kinds of pressure or force, if any, were used on you? (READ THE LIST AND CIRCLE THE APPROPRIATE RESPONSES.)

YES	NO		
2	1	(1)	Verbal persuasion, such as "If you love me, you will" or "I'll break up with you if you don't"
2	1	(2)	Verbal threats to tell others of the event or something embarrassing or bad about you
2	1	(3)	Verbal threats of injury
2	1	(4)	The person(s) was bigger and stronger
2	1	(5)	There was more than one person
2	1	(6)	I was drugged or gotten drunk
2	1	(7)	I was taken by surprise such as being asleep
2	1	(8)	Pushing, slapping and mild roughness
2	1	(9)	Display of a weapon such as a knife, bottle or cigarette lighter
2	1	(10)	Physical beating and/or choking
2	1	(11)	Injury from a weapon such as cutting with a knife or burned by a lighter
2	1	(12)	Other (SPECIFY) _____

413. What did you do or say, if anything, to try to stop the person(s)? (DO NOT READ THE FOLLOWING LISTS. CHECK ALL THAT APPLY. IF RESPONDENT SAYS "I didn't do anything," ASK: Why?)

TYPES OF RESISTANCE

    ____ (1) I reasoned with the offender(s) or talked my way out of it.
    ____ (2) I used an excuse such as "I'm pregnant," "I'm having my period," "I'm underage," or "I have a venereal disease."
    ____ (3) I got hostile or angry, told the offender(s) I wouldn't stand for it.
    ____ (4) I screamed and yelled, made noise.
    ____ (5) I physically resisted and fought back.
    ____ (6) I ran away.
    ____ (7) I couldn't control myself, became hysterical, "lost it," etc.
    ____ (8) Other (SPECIFY) _____

Appendix C

REASONS FOR NON-RESISTANCE

    ____ (1) I was scared and/or afraid
    ____ (2) I was intimidated or frightened because of my relationship with the offender(s).
    ____ (3) I was drunk or high.
    ____ (4) Other (SPECIFY) _____

414. Were you able to stop the person(s)?

Yes	No	Other factors stopped the person(s) such as interruption by others, etc.
2	1	3

415. In your opinion, how much did the following things contribute, if at all, to the event happening? Choose your answers from Card number 11, the second white card. (READ THE FOLLOWING LIST AND RECORD A RESPONSE FOR EACH ITEM.)

How much did each contribute to the event happening?	Not at All	Very Little	Some	Quite A Bit	A Great Deal	(DON'T KNOW)
The location such as a dark street or place without many people around	1	2	3	4	5	____
The time of day	1	2	3	4	5	____
The type of activity in which you were involved such as partying, hitchhiking, etc.	1	2	3	4	5	____
Your being drunk or high	1	2	3	4	5	____
Your clothes, jewelry or make-up	1	2	3	4	5	____
Your flirting or teasing	1	2	3	4	5	____
Your physical build	1	2	3	4	5	____
Your being sexually excited	1	2	3	4	5	____
The person(s) being drunk or high	1	2	3	4	5	____
The person(s) had a violent personality	1	2	3	4	5	____

	Not at All	Very Little	Some	Quite A Bit	A Great Deal	(DON'T KNOW)
The person(s) had emotional problems	1	2	3	4	5	____
The person(s) being sexually excited	1	2	3	4	5	____
The type of activity in which the person(s) was involved such as partying, being out with friends, etc.	1	2	3	4	5	____
Other (SPECIFY)_____	1	2	3	4	5	____

416a.   Did you report the event to the police?

    No   Yes   Reported by someone else   (SKIP TO QUESTION 418, PAGE 80)
    1   2   3

416b.   Could you tell me why you made the decision you did?

IF YES, REASONS FOR REPORTING   (DO NOT READ THE LIST. CHECK ALL THAT APPLY.)

____ (1) I was afraid of the person and thought the police would help to protect me.
____ (2) I trusted the police to handle the case effectively and with consideration.
____ (3) To prevent the person from doing it again.
____ (4) Other (SPECIFY) _____

(SKIP TO QUESTION 417, PAGE 80)

IF NO, REASONS FOR NOT REPORTING   (DO NOT READ LIST. CHECK ALL THAT APPLY.)

____ (1) I felt the police wouldn't believe me.
____ (2) I was afraid the police would be insensitive or mistreat me.
____ (3) I was scared the person might retaliate if I reported.
____ (4) I was embarrassed or ashamed.
____ (5) I was afraid my family and/or friends would react unfavorably toward me.
____ (6) I knew the person well or I had a relationship with the person.
____ (7) I was drunk or high.
____ (8) I wasn't hurt; the person didn't do anything; no harm done.
____ (9) Because I believe that rapists are rarely caught or convicted.
____ (10) Other (SPECIFY) _____

(SKIP TO QUESTION 418, PAGE 80)

Appendix C

417. How did the police respond to your report? Choose your answers from Card number 12, the second tan card. Look at the first set, would you say the police . . .

(1)	Were Concerned About You 1	Were Somewhat Concerned About You 2	Were Neither Concerned nor Unconcerned About You 3	Were Somewhat Unconcerned About You 4	Were Unconcerned About You 5
(2)	Believed You 1	Somewhat Believed You 2	Neither Believed Nor Disbelieved You 3	Somewhat Disbelieved You 4	Disbelieved You 5
(3)	Handled the Report Efficiently 1	Handled the Report Somewhat Efficiently 2	Handled the Report Neither Efficiently nor Inefficiently 3	Handled the Report Somewhat Inefficiently 4	Handled the Report Inefficiently 5
(4)	Were Sensitive To You 1	Were Somewhat Sensitive To You 2	Were Neither Sensitive nor Insensitive To You 3	Were Somewhat Insensitive To You 4	Were Insensitive To You 5

418. At the time of the event, were you . . .(READ LIST; RECORD RESPONSE.)

    ____ (1) Married
    ____ (2) Living with someone
    ____ (3) Going with a special boyfriend/girlfriend
    ____ (4) None of the above

(IF (4), SKIP TO QUESTION 422, PAGE 82)

(TURN TO PAGE 76: CHECK ITEM 410. WAS THE OFFENDER THE HUSBAND/WIFE/BOYFRIEND/GIRLFRIEND?)

    Yes   No   (IF NO, SKIP TO QUESTION 419, PAGE 81)
    2   1

Has your relationship changed as a result of the event?

    Yes   No   (IF NO, SKIP TO QUESTION 422, PAGE 82)
    2   1

How has your relationship changed?
(PROBE TO GET AS SPECIFIC A DESCRIPTION AS POSSIBLE.)

_____

_____

(SKIP TO QUESTION 422, PAGE 82)

419. Did you tell your _____ (husband/wife/boyfriend/girlfriend) about the event?

| Yes | No | Did your _____ (husband/wife/boyfriend/
| 2 | 1 | girlfriend) learn about the event from some other source?

| | | Yes | No (IF NO, SKIP TO QUESTION 422,
| | | 2 | 1   PAGE 82)

420. Which of the following statements, if any, describe your _____ (husband's/wife's/boyfriend's/girlfriend's) initial reactions upon learning about the event?
(READ THE LIST AND CIRCLE THE APPROPRIATE RESPONSES.)

YES NO

2	1	(1)	Shocked
2	1	(2)	Concerned about you
2	1	(3)	Supportive of you
2	1	(4)	Fearful for you
2	1	(5)	Angry at the person(s) who pushed or forced sex on you
2	1	(6)	Did not believe you
2	1	(7)	Angry at you
2	1	(8)	Blamed you
2	1	(9)	Rejected you
2	1	(10)	Other (SPECIFY) _____

421. Which of the following statements, if any, describe changes in your relationship with your _____ (husband/wife/boyfriend/girlfriend) as a result of the event? (READ THE LIST AND CIRCLE THE APPROPRIATE RESPONSES.)

YES NO

2	1	(1)	Closer than before
2	1	(2)	Not as close as before
2	1	(3)	More protective of you
2	1	(4)	Less protective of you
2	1	(5)	More trusting of you
2	1	(6)	Less trusting of you
2	1	(7)	Think more of you because of the event
2	1	(8)	Think less of you because of the event
2	1	(9)	More affectionate than before
2	1	(10)	Less affectionate than before
2	1	(11)	Other (SPECIFY) _____

Appendix C   165

422. Did you tell your parents about the event?

    Yes   No   Did your parents learn about the event from some other
    2   1   source?

                         Yes   No   (IF NO, SKIP TO QUESTION 425)
                         2   1

423. Which of the following statements, if any, describe your parents' initial reactions upon learning of the event? (READ THE LIST AND CIRCLE THE APPROPRIATE RESPONSES.)

YES	NO		
2	1	(1)	Shocked
2	1	(2)	Concerned about you
2	1	(3)	Supportive of you
2	1	(4)	Fearful for you
2	1	(5)	Angry at the person(s) who pushed or forced sex on you
2	1	(6)	Did not believe you
2	1	(7)	Angry at you
2	1	(8)	Blamed you
2	1	(9)	Other (SPECIFY)_____

424. Which of the following statements, if any describe changes in your relationship with your parents as a result of the event? (READ THE LIST AND CIRCLE THE APPROPRIATE RESPONSES.)

YES	NO		
2	1	(1)	Closer than before
2	1	(2)	Not as close as before
2	1	(3)	More protective of you
2	1	(4)	Less protective of you
2	1	(5)	More trusting of you
2	1	(6)	Less trusting of you
2	1	(7)	Think more of you because of the event
2	1	(8)	Think less of you because of the event
2	1	(9)	Other (SPECIFY) _____

425. Do any of your close friends know about the event?

                Yes   No   (IF NO, SKIP TO QUESTION 427, PAGE 83)
                2   1

426. Which of the following statements, if any, describe their reactions? (READ THE LIST AND CIRCLE THE APPROPRIATE RESPONSES.)

YES	NO		
2	1	(1)	Concerned about you
2	1	(2)	Embarrassed by you
2	1	(3)	Angry at the person(s) who pushed or forced sex on you
2	1	(4)	Fearful for you and/or themselves
2	1	(5)	Angry at you
2	1	(6)	Supportive of you
2	1	(7)	Less friendly toward you
2	1	(8)	Became closer to you
2	1	(9)	Other (SPECIFY) _____

427. Now I'd like to ask about your involvement in certain community and school activities. First, I will ask whether you were involved in each one before the event happened. Then, if you were, I will ask whether there was any change in your involvement as a result of the event. (READ EACH ITEM AND CIRCLE YES OR NO. IF NO, GO ON TO THE NEXT ITEM AND IF YES, RECORD RESPONSE IN THE SECOND COLUMN.)

		Were you involved in each before the event?		Did your involvement increase, decrease or stay the same after the event?			
		No	Yes	Increase	About the Same	Decrease	(DON'T KNOW)
(1)	a job?	1	2	3	2	1	_____
(2)	community activities such as service clubs, hobby clubs or religious groups?	1	2	3	2	1	_____
(3)	school athletics?	1	2	3	2	1	_____
(4)	Other school activities such as clubs, yearbook, school newspaper?	1	2	3	2	1	_____
(5)	social activities such as dating, parties or dances?	1	2	3	2	1	_____
(6)	spending time with other students such as between classes and after school?	1	2	3	2	1	_____
(7)	your studies?	1	2	3	2	1	_____

Appendix C

428. Did you stop going to school for awhile or quit because of the event?

　　　　No　　　Yes, stopped for awhile　　　Yes, quit
　　　　1　　　　　　　　2　　　　　　　　　　3

　　　　(IF EITHER YES RESPONSE, SKIP TO QUESTION 430)

429. Were you enrolled in school at the time of the event? (RECORD AS YES IF DURING SCHOOL VACATION.)

　　　　Yes　　No
　　　　2　　　1

430. Did you talk with any of the following people about this event? (READ EACH ITEM AND CIRCLE YES OR NO. IF NO, GO ON TO THE NEXT ITEM AND IF YES, RECORD RESPONSE IN THE SECOND COLUMN, SAYING:) Please look at Card number 11, the second white card, and select the answer that best describes how much you feel the _____ helped you.

		No	Yes	Not at All	Very Little	Some	Quite A Bit	A Great Deal	(DON'T KNOW)
(1)	School personnel such as a teacher or school counselor	1	2	1	2	3	4	5	____
(2)	Counselor at a crisis center such as a rape or assault center or hotline	1	2	1	2	3	4	5	____
(3)	Medical doctor	1	2	1	2	3	4	5	____
(4)	Psychiatrist	1	2	1	2	3	4	5	____
(5)	Relative(s) other than parents (SPECIFY) _____	1	2	1	2	3	4	5	____
(6)	Friends	1	2	1	2	3	4	5	____
(7)	Other (SPECIFY) _____	1	2	1	2	3	4	5	____

431. Which of the following statements, if any, describe your feelings within a week of the event? (READ THE LIST AND CIRCLE THE APPROPRIATE RESPONSES.)

YES   NO

YES	NO		
2	1	(1)	Fearful that the person(s) would return
2	1	(2)	Fearful of other men
2	1	(3)	Fearful of other women
2	1	(4)	Fearful of being alone
2	1	(5)	Fearful of having sex again
2	1	(6)	Felt guilty about the event
2	1	(7)	Felt embarrassed about the event
2	1	(8)	Felt depressed about the event
2	1	(9)	Felt angry about the event
2	1	(10)	Felt that I was worth less as a person because of the event
2	1	(11)	Not interested in having sex again
2	1	(12)	Any other feelings? (SPECIFY)_____

432. Which of the following statements, if any, describe your present feelings about the event? (READ THE LIST AND CIRCLE THE APPROPRIATE RESPONSES.)

YES   NO

YES	NO		
2	1	(1)	Fearful that the person(s) will return
2	1	(2)	Fearful of other men
2	1	(3)	Fearful of other women
2	1	(4)	Fearful of being alone
2	1	(5)	Fearful of having sex again
2	1	(6)	Feel guilty about the event
2	1	(7)	Feel embarrassed about the event
2	1	(8)	Feel depressed about the event
2	1	(9)	Feel angry about the event
2	1	(10)	Feel that I was worth less as a person because of the event
2	1	(11)	Not interested in having sex again
2	1	(12)	Any other feelings? (SPECIFY)_____

(PLEASE THANK THE RESPONDENT BY SAYING:)
We want you to know that we appreciate your willingness to share a personal experience with us. This sheet expresses our thanks and offers information on local resources should you want to talk further about your experience.

(OFFER DEBRIEFING SHEET TO RESPONDENT.)

(DID THE RESPONDENT REQUEST COUNSELING INFORMATION?)

        YES   NO

Appendix C   169

We've now completed the formal part of the interview, but I'd like to give you a chance to add comments to the information you've already given me.

433. Would you like to explain any of your answers further? _____
_____
_____

434. Were there any specific questions I asked that made you feel particularly uncomfortable?

   (IF YES, WHICH ONES?)_____
   _____
   _____

435. What questions would you ask if you really wanted to learn about people your age?

   _____
   _____
   _____

436. Do you think that we will have a good or poor understanding of your relationship with your family and friends from your answers to these questions?

                    Good Understanding   Poor Understanding
                            1   2

   Comments:_____
   _____
   _____

Thank you very much for your participation in this study. As in past years, there is a possibility that you may be contacted in a few weeks for a short follow-up interview.

Debriefing Sheet for Sexual Assault Victims

We appreciate that you have talked with us about this experience. Your willingness to share your personal feelings will help us to better understand why and how such behavior occurs and what kind of impact it may have on young people.

If talking about your experience has raised any concerns and you would like to further discuss some of your feelings, we have a list of counseling services available in your area. Please let the interviewer know if you would like a list of these services.

Bibliography

Abel, G.G.; Blanchard, E.B.; and Becker, J.V. "An Integrated Treatment Program for Rapists." In *Clinical Aspects of the Rapist*, edited by R. Roda. New York: Grune and Stratton, 1978.

Abel, G.G.; Madden, D.; and Christopher, R. "The Components of Rapists' Sexual Arousal." Paper presented at the American Psychiatric Association, New York, August 1975.

Adler, F. *Sisters in Crime*. New York: McGraw-Hill, 1975.

Alan Guttmacher Institute. *Teenage Pregnancy: The Problem That Hasn't Gone Away*. New York: Alan Guttmacher Institute, 1981.

Amir, M. "Victim Precipitated Forcible Rape." *Journal of Criminal Law, Criminology and Police Science* 58 (1967):493.

———. *Patterns in Forcible Rape*. Chicago: University of Chicago Press, 1971.

Blanchard, W.H. "The Group Process in Gang Rape." *Journal of Social Psychology* 49 (1959):259–266.

Bohmer, C. "Judicial Attitudes toward Rape Victims." *Judicature* 58 (February 1974):303–307.

Broverman, I.K.; Vogel, S.R.; Broverman, D.M.; Clarkson, F.E.; and Rosenkrantz, P.S. "Sex-role Stereotypes: A Current Appraisal." *Journal of Social Issues* 28 (1972):59–78.

Brownmiller, S. *Against Our Will: Men, Women and Rape*. New York: Simon and Schuster, 1975.

Burgess, A.W., and Holmstrom, L.L. *Rape: Victims of Crisis*. Bowie, Md.: Robert J. Brady Company, 1974.

Burt, M.R. "Cultural Myths and Supports for Rape." *Journal of Personality and Social Psychology* 38 (1980):217–230.

Cann, A.; Calhoun, L.G.; and Shelby, J.W. "Sexual Experience as a Factor in Reactions to Rape Victims." Paper presented at the meetings of the American Psychological Association, San Francisco, August 1977.

Catlin, G., and Murray, S. *Report on Canadian Victimization Survey Methodological Pretests*. Ottawa: Statistics Canada, 1979.

Chafetz, J.S. *Masculine/Feminine or Human?* Itasca, Ill.: Peacock, 1974.

Clark, J.P., and Tifft, L.L. "Polygraph and Interview Validation of Self-Reported Deviant Behavior." *American Sociological Review* 31 (1966):516–523.

Clark, J.P., and Wenninger, E.P. "Socio-economic Class and Area as Correlates of Illegal Behavior among Juveniles." *American Sociological Review* 27 (1962):826–834.

Cloward, R., and Ohlin, L.E. *Delinquency and Opportunity: A Theory of Delinquent Gangs.* Glencoe, Ill.: Free Press, 1960.

Cressey, P. *Other People's Money.* New York: Free Press, 1953.

Cronbach, L.J. "Alpha and the Internal Structure of Tests." *Psychometrika* 16 (1951):297–334.

Curtis, L.A. *Criminal Violence.* Lexington, Mass.: Lexington Books, D.C. Heath and Company, 1974.

———."Rape, Race and Culture: Some Speculation in Search of a Theory." In *Sexual Assault: The Victim and the Rapist*, edited by M.J. Walker and S.L. Brodsky, pp. 117–134. Lexington, Mass.: Lexington Books, D.C. Heath and Company, 1976.

Deming, M.B., and Eppy, A. "The Sociology of Rape." *Sociology and Social Research* 65 (1981):357–380.

Dentler, R.A., and Monroe, L.J. "Social Correlates of Early Adolescent Theft." *American Sociological Review* 26 (1961):733–743.

Dodge, R.W. "Victim Recall Pretest—Washington, D.C." Washington, D.C.: U.S. Census Bureau Memorandum, June 10, 1970.

Dodge, R.W., and Turner, A.G. "Methodological Foundations for Establishing a National Survey of Victimization." Paper presented at the meetings of the American Statistical Association, Fort Collins, Colorado, 1971.

Eisenhower, M.S. *To Establish Justice, to Insure Domestic Tranquility.* Final Report of the National Commission on Causes and Prevention of Violence. Washington, D.C.: U.S. Government Printing Office, December 1969.

Elliott, D.S.; Huizinga, D.; and Ageton, S.S. *Explaining Delinquency and Drug Use.* National Youth Survey, Project Report No. 21. Boulder, Colo.: Behavioral Research Institute, July 1982.

Elliott D.S., and Voss, H.L. *Delinquency and Dropout.* Lexington, Mass.: Lexington Books, D.C. Heath and Company, 1974.

Elliott, D.S.; Ageton, S.S.; and Canter, R.J. "An Integrated Theoretical Perspective on Delinquent Behavior." *Journal of Research in Crime and Delinquency* 16 (January 1979):3–27.

Elliott, D.S.; Ageton, S.S.; Huizinga, D.; Knowles, B.; and Canter, R.J. *The Prevalence and Incidence of Delinquent Behavior: 1976–1980.* National Youth Survey, Project Report No. 26. Boulder, Colo.: Behavioral Research Institute, March 1983.

Evrard, J.R., and Gold, E.M. "Epidemiology and Management of Sexual Assault Victims." *Obstetrics and Gynecology* 53 (March 1979):381–387.

Fattah, E.A. "The Use of the Victim as an Agent of Self-legitimization: Toward a Dynamic Explanation of Criminal Behavior." In *Victims and Society*, edited by E.C. Viano. Washington, D.C.: Visage Press, 1976.

Bibliography

Feldman-Summers, S.A. "Rape Reporting: Causes and Consequences." Grant application to the National Center for the Prevention and Control of Rape, 1975.

———. "Research Study on Rape Victims." Mimeographed. Grant funded by the National Center for the Prevention and Control of Rape (1RO1 MH26130), 1976.

Flanagan, T.J.; Hindelang, M.J.; and Gottfredson, M., eds. *Sourcebook of Criminal Justice Statistics—1979*. U.S. Law Enforcement Assistance Administration, National Criminal Justice Information and Statistics Service. Washington, D.C.: U.S. Government Printing Office, 1980.

Flanagan, T.J.; van Alstyne, D.J.; and Gottfredson, M.R., eds. *Sourcebook of Criminal Justice Statistics—1981*. U.S. Law Enforcement Assistance Administration, National Criminal Justice Information and Statistics Service. Washington, D.C.: U.S. Government Printing Office, 1982.

Fotjik, K.M. "Ann Arbor Overview." *National Organization for Women—Ann Arbor* 9 (1976).

Friedan, B. *The Feminine Mystique*. New York: Dell Publishing, 1963.

Gager, N., and Schurr, C. *Sexual Assault: Confronting Rape in America*. New York: Grosset and Dunlap, 1976.

Garofalo, J., and Hindelang, M. *An Introduction to the National Crime Survey*. U.S. Department of Justice, Law Enforcement Assistance Administration. Washington, D.C.: U.S. Government Printing Office, 1977.

Gebhard, P.H.; Pomeroy, W.B.; Martin, C.E.; and Christenson, C.V. *Pregnancy, Birth and Abortion*. New York: Harper and Brothers, 1958.

Geller, S.H. "The Sexually Assaulted Female: Innocent Victim or Temptress?" *Canada's Mental Health* 25 (March 1977):26–29.

Gibbons, D.C. "Forcible Rape: Current Knowledge and Research Issues." Paper presented at the American Society of Criminology, Toronto, November 1982.

Gold, M. "Undetected Delinquent Behavior." *Journal of Research in Crime and Delinquency* 3 (1966):27–46.

Greenberg, M.S., and Wilson, C. "A New Methodological Approach to Investigating Victims' Reporting of a Crime." Mimeographed. Pittsburgh: University of Pittsburgh, 1977.

Griffin, S. "Rape: The All-American Crime." *Ramparts* 10 (September 1971):26–35.

Hardt, R.H., and Bodine, G.E. *Development of Self-report Instruments in Delinquency and Research*. Syracuse: Syracuse University Youth Development Center, 1965.

Hardt, R.H., and Peterson-Hardt, S. "On Determining the Quality of the Delinquency Self-report Method." *Journal of Research in Crime and Delinquency* 14 (July 1977):247–261.

Hayman, C. "Roundtable: Rape and Its Consequences." *Medical Aspects of Human Sexuality* 10 (1972):152–161.

Hayman, C.R.; Lewis, F.R.; Stewart, W.F.; and Grant, M. "Sexual Assault on Women and Children in the District of Columbia." *Public Health Reports* 83 (December 1968):1021–1028.

Hindelang, M.J.; Hirschi, T.; and Weis, J.G. *Measuring Delinquency.* Beverly Hills, Calif.: Sage Publications, 1981.

Hollingshead, A.B., and Redlich, F.C. *Social Class and Mental Illness.* New York: John Wiley, 1958.

Huizinga, D., and Elliott, D.S. "A Preliminary Examination of the Reliability and Validity of the National Youth Survey Self-Reported Delinquency Indices." Mimeographed. National Youth Survey, Project Report No. 27. Boulder, Colo.: Behavioral Research Institute, 1983.

Hursch, C.J., and Selkin, J. "Rape Prevention Research Project." Mimeographed. Annual Report of the Violence Research Unit. Denver: Department of Health and Hospitals, Division of Psychiatric Service, 1974.

Jones, C., and Aronson, E. "Attribution of Fault to a Rape Victim as a Function of Respectability of the Victim." *Journal of Personality and Social Psychology* 26 (1973):415–419.

Kalven, H., and Zeisel, H. *The American Jury.* Boston: Little, Brown, 1966.

Kanin, E.J. "Reference Groups and Sex Conduct Norm Violation." *Sociological Quarterly* 8 (1967a):495–504.

―――. "An Examination of Sexual Aggression as a Response to Sexual Frustration." *Journal of Marriage and the Family* 28 (August 1967b): 428–433.

Kanin, E.J., and Parcell, S.R. "Sexual Aggression: A Second Look at the Offended Female." *Archives of Sexual Behavior* 6 (1977):67–76.

Katz, S., and Mazur, M.A. *Understanding the Rape Victim: A Synthesis of Research Findings.* New York: John Wiley, 1979.

Kirkpatrick, C., and Kanin, E.J. "Male Sex Aggression on a University Campus." *American Sociological Review* 22 (1957):52–58.

Konopka, G. *Young Girls: A Portrait of Adolescence.* Englewood Cliffs, N.J.: Prentice-Hall, 1976.

Koss, M.P. "Hidden Rape on a University Campus." Mimeographed. Final Report on Grant No. MH31618. Rockville, Md.: National Center for the Prevention and Control of Rape, 1981.

L'Armand, K., and Pepitone, A. "On Attribution of Responsibility and Punishment for Rape." Paper presented at the meetings of the American Psychological Association, San Francisco, August 1977.

LaFree, G.D. "Official Reactions to Social Problems: Police Decisions in Sexual Assault Cases." *Social Problems* 28 (1981):582–594.

Lee, B. "Precautions against Rape." *Sexual Behavior* 2 (January 1972): 28–30.
McCahill, T.W.; Meyer, L.C.; and Fischman, A.M. *The Aftermath of Rape*. Lexington, Mass.: Lexington Books, D.C. Heath and Company, 1979.
McCombie, S.L. "Characteristics of Rape Victims Seen in Crisis Intervention." *Smith College Studies in Social Work* 46 (March 1976):137–158.
MacDonald, J.M. *Rape Offenders and Their Victims*. Springfield, Ill.: Charles C. Thomas, 1971.
Martin, D. *Battered Wives*. San Francisco: Glide Publications, 1976.
Matza, P. *Delinquency and Drift*. New York: John Wiley, 1964.
Miller, P.Y., and Simon, W. "Adolescent Sexual Behavior: Context and Change." *Social Problems* 22 (1974):58–76.
———. "The Development of Sexuality in Adolescence." In *Handbook of Adolescent Psychology*, edited by J. Adelson. New York: John Wiley, 1980.
Millett, K. *Sexual Politics*. Garden City, N.Y.: Doubleday, 1970.
Nelson, S., and Amir, M. "The Hitchhike Victim of Rape: A Research Report." In *Victimology: A New Focus*, edited by I. Drapkin and E. Viano. Lexington, Mass.: Lexington Books, D.C. Heath and Company, 1975.
Nye, F.I., and Short, J.F., Jr. "Scaling Delinquent Behaviors." *American Sociological Review* 22 (June 1957):326–331.
Peters, J.J.; Meyers, L.C.; and Carroll, N.E. *Victims of Rape*. Washington, D.C.: U.S. Government Printing Office, 1976.
Pizzey, E. *Scream Quietly or the Neighbors Will Hear*. Middlesex: Penguin Books, 1974.
Polk, K.; Adler, C.; Bazemore, G.; Blake, G.; Cordray, S.; Coventry, G.; Galvin, J.; and Temple, M. *Becoming Adult: An Analysis of Maturational Development from Age 16 to 30 of a Cohort of Young Men*. Final Report of the Marion County Youth Survey. Eugene: University of Oregon, 1981.
Pope, D. "Rape Survey of Michigan Police." Paper presented at the Seminar for the International Association of Women Police, Kalamazoo, Michigan, October 1974.
Reiss, A.J., and Rhodes, A.L. *A Sociopsychological Study of Conforming and Deviating Behavior among Adolescents*. Iowa City: University of Iowa, 1959.
Rich, A. *Of Women Born*. New York: W.W. Norton, 1976.
Robert, P. *Les bandes d'adolescents*. Paris: Ed. Ouvrières, 1966.
Russell, D.E.H. *The Politics of Rape*. New York: Stein and Day, 1975.
Sanday, P.R. "The Socio-cultural Context of Rape: A Cross-cultural Study." *Journal of Social Issues* 37 (1981):5–27.
Schneider, A.L. *Portland Forward Records Check of Crime Victims: Final Report*. Eugene, Ore.: Institute for Policy Analysis, 1977.

Schultz, L.G., and DeSavage J. "Rape and Rape Attitudes on a College Campus." In *Rape Victimology*, edited by L. Schultz. Springfield, Ill.: Charles Thomas, 1975.

Schwendinger, H., and Schwendinger, J. "Delinquent Stereotypes of Probable Victims." In *Juvenile Gangs in Context*, edited by M. W. Klein. Englewood Cliffs, N.J.: Prentice-Hall, 1967.

Scott, M.B., and Lyman, S.M. "Accounts." *American Sociological Review* 33 (February 1968):46–61.

Scott, W.A. "Attitude Measurement." In *The Handbook of Social Psychology*, 2d ed., edited by G. Lindzey and E. Aronson. Reading, Mass.: Addison-Wesley, 1968.

Scully, D., and Marolla, J. "Convicted Rapist's Attitudes toward Women and Rape." Mimeographed. 1982.

Skogan, W.G. *Issues in the Measurement of Victimization*. Washington, D.C.: Bureau of Justice Statistics, U.S. Department of Justice, 1981.

Smithyman, S.D. "The Undetected Rapist." Ph.D. dissertation, Claremont Graduate School, 1978.

Sparks, R.F.; Glenn, H.G.; and Dodd, D.J. *Surveying Victims: A Study of the Measurement of Criminal Victimization*. New York: John Wiley, 1977.

Sutherland, E.H. *Principles of Criminology*. 4th ed. Philadelphia: Lippincott, 1947.

Sykes, G.H., and Matza, D. "Techniques for Neutralization: A Theory of Delinquency." *American Sociological Review* 22 (December 1957): 664–670.

Tolor, A. "Women's Attitudes toward Forcible Rape." Mimeographed. Fairfield, Conn.: Fairfield University, 1977.

Turner, A.G. *The San Jose Methods Test of Known Crime Victims*. Washington, D.C.: National Criminal Justice Information and Statistics Service, Law Enforcement Assistance Administration, U.S. Department of Justice, 1972.

U.S. Bureau of the Census. "Estimates of the Population of the United States, by Age, Race, and Sex: 1976 to 1979." Current Population Reports Series P-25, No. 870. Washington, D.C.: U.S. Government Printing Office, 1980.

U.S. Congress. Senate. Committee on the Judiciary. *Challenge for the Third Century: Education in a Safe Environment-Final Report on the Nature and Prevention of School Violence and Vandalism*. Subcommittee to Investigate Juvenile Delinquency, 95th Cong., 1st sess., Committee Print. Washington, D.C.: U. S. Government Printing Office, 1977.

U.S. Department of Justice. *Criminal Victimization in the United States, 1973–1978 Trends*. Bureau of Justice Statistics. National Crime Survey Report NCS-N-13, NCJ-66716. Washington, D.C.: U.S. Government Printing Office, 1980.

U.S. Department of Justice. *Criminal Victimization in the United States, 1978.* Bureau of Justice Statistics. National Crime Survey Report NCS-N-17, NCJ-66480. Washington, D.C.: U.S. Government Printing Office, 1980.

U.S. Department of Justice. *Criminal Victimization in the United States, 1979.* Bureau of Justice Statistics. National Crime Survey Report NCJ-76710, NCS-N-19. Washington, D.C.: U.S. Government Printing Office, 1981.

U.S. Department of Justice. *Uniform Crime Reports.* Federal Bureau of Investigation. Washington, D.C.: U.S. Government Printing Office, 1977–1980.

Voss, H.L. "Ethnic Differentials in Delinquency in Honolulu." *Journal of Criminal Law, Criminology and Police Science* 54 (1963):322–327.

Weis, K., and Borges, S.S. "Victimology and Rape: The Case of the Legitimate Victim." *Issues in Criminology* 8 (1973):71–115.

Weitzman, L.J. "Sex-role Socialization." In *A Feminist Perspective*, edited by J. Freeman. Palo Alto, Calif.: Mayfield, 1975.

Williams, J.E., and Holmes, K.A. *The Second Assault: Rape and Public Attitudes.* Westport, Conn.: Greenwood Press, 1981.

Wolfgang, M. *Patterns in Criminal Homicide.* Philadelphia: University of Pennsylvania Press, 1958.

Wolfgang, M., and Ferracuti, F. *The Subculture of Violence.* London: Tavistock, 1967.

Yost, L.R., and Dodge, R.W. "Household Survey of Victims of Crime: Second Pretest-Baltimore, Maryland." Washington, D.C.: U.S. Census Bureau memorandum, November 30, 1970.

Zellman, G.L.; Goodchilds, J.D.; Johnson, P.B.; and Giarusso, R. "Teenagers Application of the Label 'Rape' to Nonconsensual Sex between Acquaintances." Paper presented at the American Psychological Association Meetings, Los Angeles, August 1981.

Zelnik, M., and Kantner, J.F. "Sexual and Contraceptive Experience of Young Unmarried Women in the United States, 1976 and 1971." In *Teenage Sexuality, Pregnancy, and Childbearing*, edited by F.F. Furstenberg, Jr., R. Lincoln, and J. Menken. Philadelphia: University of Pennsylvania Press, 1981.

Glossary

Birth Cohort A group of persons born in a given period of time, usually a calendar year.

Chi-square (X^2) A numerical distribution often used in tests of hypotheses about statistical independence and goodness of fit, especially when the variables involved are proportions or frequency counts. In this book, the chi-square distribution is used in tests of statistical independence. A significant chi-square value indicates that the independence hypothesis can be rejected in favor of the hypothesis that the two variables involved are dependent on each other; that is, knowing a person's classification on one variable permits a better classification on the other variable. In this book, a test of independence based on the chi-square distribution is called a *chi-square test*.

Confidence Interval An interval about a statistic (a mean or proportion, for example) that is likely to contain the true population value being estimated by the statistic. The confidence intervals used in this book are 95 percent confidence intervals; that is, if many probability samples were drawn from the population sampled, in 95 out of 100 such samples the confidence intervals established would contain the true population value. The level of error associated with this interval is thus 5 percent.

Design Effect A measure of the effect of sample clustering on estimates of the variance of a statistic. Technically it is the ratio of the observed variance of some estimate in a cluster sample to the variance of the estimate that would have been obtained in a simple random sample of the same size.

Discriminant Analysis A statistical technique that permits the study of differences between two or more groups of objects with respect to several variables simultaneously. This analysis distinguishes between groups on the basis of the variable profiles of the members of each group. The mathematical objective is to weight and linearly combine the chosen variables so that the groups are forced to be as statistically distinct as possible.

Formal Estimates Delinquency or victimization rates that are generalized to the population sampled and include a statement about the statistical accuracy of the estimated rates. Formal estimates typically include a confidence interval for the estimate—in the case of SAP estimates, a .95 confidence interval.

Incidence Rate A ratio of the number of offenses or victimizations per some population base. The rate is normally for a specified time interval (for example, monthly, annually, over one's lifetime) and may be expressed as an average number of offenses per person, per 100 persons, per 1,000 persons, or some larger population base. The offenses counted for the SAP incidence rate involve person-reported offenses rather than offense events.

Loss Rate   The percentage of persons included in the sample who did not participate (were not interviewed) in a given year. The initial loss rate refers to the percentage of persons drawn in the sample who refused to participate in the study or could not be contacted for an interview on the first survey. The loss rate for the second through fifth surveys is the percentage of participating respondents (those agreeing to be in the study and completing interviews on the first survey) who failed to complete an interview during that particular survey.

Mean, (X), Arithmetic Mean   A measure of central tendency—that is, the balancing point of a frequency distribution. It is often referred to as the average score or value. It is calculated by dividing the sum of all the observed values of a variable by the number of observed values (or cases).

Multistage Sampling   A sampling procedure that moves through a set of stages from more inclusive to less inclusive sampling units.

N   A symbol that denotes the sample size or number of cases (subjects) in an analysis.

NS (Nonsignificant)   *See* Statistically Significant.

National Crime Survey (NCS)   An annual series of reports published by the Bureau of Justice Statistics on national rates of crime victimization. These data are derived from interviews with a sample of households designed to be representative of the U.S. population and involve self-reported personal and household victimizations.

p **(Probability)**   A symbol for the probability level associated with a particular test of statistical significance. For example, whenever the probability level of a t-test is less than .05, the no-difference hypothesis is rejected, and we conclude that there is a difference between the means of the two populations on this variable.

Panel Design   A research design in which a group of individuals is followed over time, for which observations or measures are obtained at two or more time locations. A panel design typically is used to observe change or developmental processes.

Population   The total set of elements or cases possessing some common specified characteristics. For the NYS, the term refers to all youth aged eleven through seventeen living in the continental United States in 1976.

Prevalence Rate   A ratio of the number of persons in a given population or group possessing a particular characteristic to the total number of persons in that population or group. In this book, prevalence refers to the percentage of persons who report any offense of a given type within a designated calendar year. The prevalence rate is an offender (persons) rate as opposed to an offending (offense) rate. The latter rate is an incidence rate.

Probability Sample A sample drawn in such a way that the probability of each subject in the population being included in the sample is known. This type of sample permits estimates of the statistical accuracy of inferences made about the population from sample data.

Recall Period The interval of time over which the respondent is asked to remember and report specific behaviors or events. The NYS and SAP used a recall period of one year. Interviews were completed between January and March of each year and respondents were asked to recall and report offenses that occurred between "Christmas a year ago and the Christmas just past."

Reliability The level of precision of a measuring instrument. An index of the amount of variable error in a measure (scale)—for example, errors that vary from one administration to another for a given person assuming no real change occurred between administrations.

Response Set A preselected and fixed set of choices the respondent can use in selecting an answer to a survey question.

SD (Standard Deviation) A statistic used to measure the degree of dispersion or spread in a distribution of scores. The standard deviation is the square root of the variance. *See* Variance.

Sample A subset of elements or cases drawn from a population of all elements or cases.

Scale A measure composed of two or more items or questions that have a logical or empirical relationship to each other.

Selective Loss Respondent loss that occurs disproportionately in certain subgroups within the total sample—for example, a disproportionate loss among blacks compared to whites (by race), among males compared to females (by sex), or lower-class compared to middle-class youth (by social class).

Self-weighting Sample A sample in which the arithmetic mean of the sample cases is a good estimate of the population mean. A selection procedure in which all of the population elements have an equal probability of selection that usually leads to a self-weighting sample. No differential weighting of elements is required to compensate for unequal probabilities of selection since the probability of selection is constant.

Statistically Significant As used in this book, the finding that a difference between two subsamples (for example, males and females, blacks and whites) is statistically significant indicates that the probability of observing a difference this large in the two subsamples, when there is no difference in their respective populations, is so low that it is reasonable to conclude that there is a true difference in the two populations. Statistical significance thus refers to a generalization of differences from samples to their populations with a known risk of error. The risk of error for generalizations in this book is always .05 or less. If the error associated with the generalization from the samples to their populations is greater than .05, the observed difference between samples is considered nonsignificant (NS), and no claim is made for a true difference in the two populations.

Status Offense Behavior that is illegal only for youth under a certain age, usually age eighteen. Examples of status offenses include truancy, running away from home, and purchasing liquor.

t **(t-test)** A statistical test used in this book to estimate the probability that a difference as large as that observed between two sample means could occur when there was no difference in the means of the two populations from which these samples were drawn. When the t-test indicates that the probability is sufficiently low (in this book ≤ .05), we reject the hypothesis that there is no difference on this variable in the two populations and conclude that there is some real difference.

Temporal Ordering An ordering of events in time; the chronological ordering of events. A causal claim requires the demonstration of a correct temporal ordering of cause and effect variables; that is, the cause must precede the effect.

Uniform Crime Reports (UCR) An annual report of arrests and offenses known to the police published by the FBI since 1930. The UCR present national rates of arrest and crimes known to police for each of eight offenses classified as index offenses, and arrest rates for over twenty other offenses.

Validity An indication that a measure (scale) describes what it was intended or designed to describe.

Variable A measurable characteristic. The major variables addressed in this book are race, social class, place of residence, age, and sexual assault.

Variance (S^2 for a sample, σ^2 for a population) A measure of the dispersion of a set of scores around their mean. The variance is the average of the squared deviations from the mean. *See* Standard Deviation.

Index

Abel, G.G., 104, 121
Adler, F., 66, 68
Ageton, S.S., 101, 102, 116
Alan Guttmacher Institute, 100
Amir, M., 3, 40, 65, 68, 92, 103, 135
Aronson, E., 68

Becker, J.V., 121
Blanchard, E.B., 121
Blanchard, W.H., 102
Bodine, G.E., 17
Bohmer, C., 68
Borges, S.S., 66, 67, 69
Broverman, I.K., 103
Brownmiller, S., 66, 67, 103
Burgess, A.W., 48
Burt, M.R., 104

Calhoun, L.G., 68
Cann, A., 68
Canter, R.J., 102
Carroll, N.E., 3
Catlin, G., 4, 12
Chafetz, J.S., 103
Christopher, R., 104, 121
Clark, J.P., 17
Cloward, R., 102
Cressey, P., 104
Cronbach, L.J., 149
Curtis, L.A., 3, 65

Deming, M.B., 6
Dentler, R.A., 17
DeSavage, J., 4
Dodd, D.J., 12, 13
Dodge, R.W., 12, 13

Eisenhower, M.S., 92, 135
Elliott, D.S., 15, 16, 17, 101, 102, 116, 151
Eppy, A., 6
Evrard, J.R., 4

Fattah, E.A., 104
Feldman-Summers, S.A., 3, 18

Ferracuti, F., 103
Fischman, A.M., 3, 34, 48, 61
Flanagan, T.J., 103
Fotjik, K.M., 103
Friedan, B., 102

Gager, N., 66, 67
Garofalo, J., 13
Gebhard, P.H., 17
Geller, S.H., 40
Gibbons, D.C., 139
Glenn, H.G., 12, 13
Gold, E.M., 4
Gold, M., 16
Gottfredson, M., 3, 18, 30, 34
Greenberg, M.S., 3
Griffin, S., 67, 103

Hardt, R.H., 17
Hayman, C., 4, 66, 68
Hindelang, M.J., 13, 16, 17, 34
Hirschi, T., 16, 17
Hollingshead, A.B., 18
Holmes, K.A., 4, 65, 67, 68, 81
Holmstrom, L.L., 48
Huizinga, D., 17, 101, 102, 116, 151
Hursch, C.J., 3

Jones, C., 68

Kalven, H., 68
Kanin, E.J., 4, 67, 93, 102, 111, 121
Katz, S., 3, 33, 80
Kirkpatrick, C., 67
Konopka, G., 68
Koss, M.P., 100, 139, 140

LaFree, G.D., 92
L'Armand, K., 68
Lee, B., 66, 68
Lyman, S.M., 104

McCahill, T.W., 3, 34, 48, 61
McCombie, S.L., 3

183

MacDonald, J.M., 3, 92, 103, 135
Madden, D., 104, 121
Marolla, J., 104
Martin, D., 103
Matza, D., 104
Mazur, M.A., 3, 33, 80
Meyer, L.C., 3, 34, 48, 61
Millett, K., 103
Monroe, L.J., 17
Murray, S., 4, 12

Nelson, S., 40, 68
Nye, F.I., 17

Ohlin, L.E., 102

Parcell, S.R., 4
Pepitone, A., 68
Peters, J.J., 3
Peterson-Hardt, S., 17
Pizzey, E., 103
Polk, K., 93, 102, 111, 121
Pope, D., 68

Redlich, F.C., 18
Reiss, A.J., 17
Rhodes, A.L., 17
Rich, A., 103
Robert, P., 68
Russell, D.E.H., 67, 68

Sanday, P.R., 4, 65
Schneider, A.L., 13, 14
Schultz, L.G., 4
Schurr, C., 66, 67
Schwendinger, H., 104

Schwendinger, J., 104
Scott, M.B., 104
Scott, W.A., 150
Scully, D., 104
Selkin, J., 3
Shelby, J.W., 68
Short, J.F., Jr., 17, 45, 60
Skogan, W.G., 13, 14
Smithyman, S.D., 93, 111
Sparks, R.F., 12, 13
Sutherland, E.H., 102
Sykes, G.H., 104

Tifft, L.L., 17
Tolor, A., 67
Turner, A.G., 4, 12, 13

U.S. Bureau of the Census, 91
U.S. Congress, 3
U.S. Department of Justice, 1980, 3

van Alstyne, D.J., 3, 18, 30, 34
Voss, H.L., 16, 17, 102

Weis, J.G., 16, 17
Weis, K., 66, 67, 69
Weitzman, L.J., 67, 103
Wenninger, E.P., 17
Williams, J.E., 4, 65, 67, 68, 81
Wilson, C., 3
Wolfgang, M.E., 103

Yost, L.R., 12

Zeisel, H., 68
Zellman, G.L., 4, 48, 100, 140

About the Author

Suzanne S. Ageton received the Ph.D. from the University of Colorado. She is a senior research associate at the Behavioral Research Institute where she is currently the co-principal investigator on an ongoing national study of delinquent behavior. Dr. Ageton was the principal investigator on the sexual-assault study that generated the data presented in this book. Recent publications include an article with Delbert S. Elliott in the February 1980 issue of *American Sociological Review* entitled "Reconciling Race and Class Differences in Self-Reported and Official Estimates of Delinquency" and an article entitled "The Dynamics of Female Delinquency, 1976–1980," forthcoming in *Criminology*.